KATRINA STANDS ALONE

Natelkka E. Burrell

Review and Herald Publishing Association
Washington, DC 20039-0555
Hagerstown, MD 21740

Copyright © 1988 by
Review and Herald Publishing Association

This book was
Edited by Gerald Wheeler
Designed by Richard Steadham

Printed in U.S.A.

Library of Congress Cataloging in Publication Data

Burrell, Natelkka E., 1895-
  Katrina stands alone/by Natelkka E. Burrell.
     p.   cm.
  ISBN 0-8280-0408-0
  1. Nesbitt, Katrina Viola, 1918- . 2. Teachers—United States—
Biography. I. Title.
LA2317.N47B87 1988
371.1'0092'4—dc19
[B]   87-32536
                                                                                  CIP

ACKNOWLEDGMENTS

To Kathy Beagles, English Department of Andrews University, who helped me with much of the writing technique, read many of the chapters, and gave valuable suggestions.

To Dorothy Minchin-Comm, English Department of Loma Linda University, who read the manuscript and suggested a reorganization for greater readability.

To Katrina, who graciously submitted to several interviews and gave approval to the contents of the manuscript.

To the many friends who constantly encouraged me to keep at the writing task.

To God, for the desire to tell Katrina's story.

I have written this book to show that a childhood of abuse does not necessarily mean one cannot rise to a life of useful purpose. Had the Hawthorne effect been fulfilled in this young woman's life, she would have been anything other than an honorable woman, determined to do all and be all her talents allowed her to be.

Her experiences have led her to have a deep interest in the odd ones—the underachiever, the slow learner, the apathetic child, and the underprivileged. She delights in working with such children and in watching them grow. She is a champion of the abused child, and it has been her privilege to see many of these "bad" children turn out well. They sometimes make mistakes but never forget what this unusual teacher has told them. Most of them develop lives that make her proud.

The names of some of the relatives have been changed to protect their privacy.

Contents

1. The Runaway — 7
2. Origins — 12
3. The Early Years — 16
4. Through the Grades — 21
5. Teenage Abuse — 30
6. On to High School — 33
7. An Adventure Into Freedom — 40
8. Teacher Goes to the Everglades — 47
9. City Bound — 55
10. Back to College — 61
11. She Said, "No!" God Said, "Yes!" — 65
12. Supervising Teacher — 68
13. More Stately Dwellings — 74
14. Northward Bound — 77
15. The Bard Experience — 84
16. Honors for a Super Teacher — 90

1

THE RUNAWAY

Silence spread a thin veil over the residential areas of Miami on that hot summer afternoon. In a house on Sixteenth Terrace, Mama Lois, wife of Andrew Nesbitt, Sr.—affectionately known as Captain Andy—busied herself with household matters. Her 4-year-old granddaughter, Katrina, whom she and her husband had adopted, played alone in the large back and side yards. The sons of Captain Andy and Lois were scattered about the neighborhood, except the oldest one, Andrew, Jr., the father of 4-year-old Katrina. Her mother had sent him to an uncle in New York City.

Often the youngest son, Joseph, played with his young niece, but on this afternoon he, too, had wandered off. Katrina had no one to play with or to talk to and when you are 4, you have so many things to say. You need someone to listen to you and play with you. The girl looked at the board fence between Mama Lois's house and that of Mrs. Graham. Then she saw the loose board and the hole big enough for her to squeeze through. The Grahams liked her—she could visit with Mrs. Graham, and perhaps Lucille, her 12-year-old daughter, would play with her, too. But Mama Lois had spanked her hard for going through that hole. Not liking Mama's spankings, she decided not to wriggle through the fence. Instead she wandered toward the front yard searching for something interesting to do. As she glimpsed the front gate, an idea formed in her mind. *I'll go see my mother,* she thought. *She'll play with me.*

Katrina pushed the gate open and stood on the sidewalk, then began walking slowly toward Third Avenue. As she passed Mrs. Graham's house, Lucille saw her and called out cheerily, "Hello, 'Trina."

7

"Hello," Katrina responded. "I'm going to see my mother."

"You can't do that. You're too little, and you don't know where she lives," Lucille countered.

"I do too know where my mother lives and I can so go there by myself," the 4-year-old said positively.

By now Lucille had come out of her yard and joined her. "Does your Mama Lois know you're going to see your mother?" the girl asked.

"Uh-uh," Katrina answered with a vigorous shake of her head.

"Oh! you're going to catch it when you get back," Lucille warned. "Want to go back and ask?"

"No! Mama would just fuss and say 'no.'"

"Well, here we are at Third Avenue. I'll take you across the street, then I'll have to leave you. I'm not allowed to leave our block."

The two girls crossed safely, then Lucille returned to their side of the avenue and watched as Katrina continued on toward Seventeenth Street and another crosswalk. Without a thought Katrina stepped off the curb and calmly started across the street when a horn blew and a car whizzed by behind her. She quickened her steps, eyes focused on the far curb when again a horn blew and a car screeched to a halt a foot or two from her. A startled and irate man yelled, "Hey you, don't you know better than to cross the street alone? Where's your mother?" Safely on the sidewalk, Katrina turned, beamed up at him, and answered, "I'm going to see my mother. Bye."

Muttering to himself about careless mothers who let their kids run wild, the man drove on. The girl happily continued her walk. Fortunately she had no more street crossings until she reached her mother's house nearly three blocks away. Katrina's plump little legs pumped the hot sidewalk as she watched for the large white house with the big green lawn and lots of pretty flowers. She knew the house—Papa had taken her there several times. Always in that house her mother, the other grown-ups, and all the children made her feel wanted and loved. Ah! There it sat just as she remembered it—white house, big green lawn, pretty flowers.

THE RUNAWAY

Great-grandmother Celeste saw her first. "Oh!" she exclaimed. "Maybelle, it is your bebe!"

Everyone in the house rushed out to greet the little traveler. Maybelle swept the tired child up in her arms, hugged her, and covered her with kisses. "My darling, who brought you here?"

"I came by myself," the child replied happily.

Maybelle's mother, Marie, wide-eyed, drew in her breath sharply as she envisioned all that might have happened.

The child's mother voiced all their fears, "Oh! Don't ever do that again. You could have been hurt, even killed. Next time wait for Papa to bring you to see us. But come now and tell us all about how you got here."

From the shelter of her mother's arms Katrina told her little saga to an admiring audience. Then she played awhile with Maybelle's younger sisters until the grandmother warned, "I know, Maybelle, you want to keep your child, but you'll have to take her back to her father's people. She's a dear little girl; I wish we could keep her."

"But, Mother—"

"No 'buts.' I dislike the idea as much as you do. However, until we can get the child legally, we'll just have to take her back."

"I know, Mother, you're right, but it's so hard. I'll take her back to Miss Lois."

"No, I'll do it," Maybelle's twin, Clarabelle, volunteered. "Or better yet, I'll watch for Captain Andy. It's almost time for him to come from work. When he passes, I'll hail him and tell him Katrina is here."

"A great idea," Maybelle declared. "Thank you, Sis. That way none of us will have to face Miss Lois's contempt, and Katrina loves Captain Andy, so there'll be no tears when she leaves."

"I'd better get outside immediately in case he gets off a bit early," Clarabelle suggested.

Captain Andy wiped his oily hands, made himself as presentable as possible, picked up his lunch pail, bade goodbye to his fellow workers, straddled his bike, and started his journey home.

KATRINA STANDS ALONE

As he drew near the Cravattes' house, he saw Clarabelle waving and signaling for him to stop.

"Hello, young lady. What's on your mind?" he questioned.

"Please come in, Mr. Nesbitt. We've a surprise for you."

"Surprise? Whatever could it be?"

"Come in and see," Clarabelle laughingly responded, leading the way up the path to the house. Before they reached the house, Maybelle appeared in the doorway with Katrina.

As soon as she saw him the child called out joyfully, "Papa," the name she had given to Captain Andy. She ran and leaped into his outstretched arms.

Hugging her close he asked, "Katrina Baby, how on earth did you get here? Who brought you?"

Head held high, eyes bright, she answered, "Nobody. I came all the way by myself."

"What!" Captain Andy cried in alarm. "Child, don't ever do that again. You could have been run over, seriously injured, or lost. Wait for me or someone to bring you here. Promise?"

"Yeah, I promise."

"Good! Now tell me how you found your way here."

"I remember when you take me, Papa. I look for the big white house and the pretty flowers."

Maybelle, her sister Clarabelle, and her mother, Marie, and great-grandmother, Celeste, all crowded around to tell how surprised they were to see their little guest. After kisses all around and a special kiss and big hug from Maybelle, Katrina turned to her grandfather, took his hand, and said, "We go home now, Papa."

"Yes, Mama will be looking for us," Captain Andy agreed.

Maybelle and her twin followed Captain Andy and the child to the gate. Papa placed Katrina carefully on his bike, leaped on himself, and continued home, whistling his favorite hymn tune, "As pants the hart for cooling streams . . ." In a short time they reached Sixteenth Terrace and home. He put his bicycle in the shed while Katrina followed him, then both entered the house.

He called out, "Lois, I'm home."

"Good. Dinner will be ready by the time you are," his wife answered.

THE RUNAWAY

Then gently he said to the child, who clung to his pant leg, "Papa's going upstairs to bathe and change. You stay here. Mama will come to you soon."

Katrina's large brown eyes followed him up the stairs. In minutes Mama Lois appeared, a frown on her face. She saw the girl standing there and asked, "Where have you been? Didn't I tell you to stay in the yard?"

Fear filled Katrina's eyes as she looked up at Mama Lois, but no words came, only a little frightened smile. Infuriated by the silent response, Mama Lois smacked the girl on both sides of her face. Still the child did not make any sound, but her eyes filled with tears. The silence further enraged her grandmother who then grasped the child and shook her as hard as she possibly could before flinging her against the wall, where Katrina fell in a crumpled heap, screaming as she fell.

Papa raced down the stairs and scooped up the sobbing child. Seeing his wife standing nearby, he demanded, "Woman, have you gone crazy? What have you done to this girl?"

Breathing deeply, eyes flashing, the woman responded, "I'll not have her disobeying and defying me, the little brat!"

"Oh, Lois, stop blaming the child for what our son did. She is innocent. If you had treated her right, she would not have wanted to run away. It's all your fault." So saying, he started up the stairs with his now-sniffling little burden.

"My fault!" Mama Lois hissed to her husband's retreating back. "My fault!" she repeated as she walked, head high, back straight, toward the kitchen. "My fault? What about that little French hussy that seduced my son? Was that my fault?"

Papa looked for bruises, bathed Katrina, and changed her rumpled clothing after putting emollients on all the sore places. Then they went down to dinner.

2

ORIGINS

Katrina Viola Nesbitt began life and grew up in an atmosphere of mingled love and disdain. Captain Andrew Nesbitt had acquired property in Miami, Florida, and built a large house in which he and his wife, Lois, raised their sons. Andrew, Jr., the oldest one, married Maybelle Cravatte, whose family had migrated from a French West Indian Island, while his parents had come from Nassau in the British West Indies. At the time, migrants from the British islands looked with disapproval upon those from other islands. The marriage of Lois Wilson to the well-to-do Captain Andrew Nesbitt gave her considerable clout among the Miamians. Naturally she held high expectations for her sons. However, the secret high school romance and ensuing marriage of her 18-year-old son to a French Caribbean girl wrecked her hopes for a high social position for him. In spite of her son's indiscretion and Maybelle's pregnancy, she opposed their marriage. Nevertheless, Captain Andy saw it as the only honorable thing to do and bade his son marry the girl, then only 15. Lois refused to attend the wedding, and when her son brought his bride home to live, his mother declared, "That hussy can't live in my house!"

Maybelle's face flushed at the announcement and tears sprang up in her eyes. Her young husband exclaimed, "Mama!"

Captain Andy, who had attended the wedding but had preceded the couple home, turned and sharply addressed his wife. "Lois, I built this house for you and our family. Any woman who marries one of our sons is a Nesbitt and is welcome as long as she chooses to stay!" Then turning to the young couple he continued, "Son, take your bride up to the guest room."

"Thanks, Papa," Junior gratefully told his father as he bent to pick up the luggage.

12

ORIGINS

In a kind voice the captain addressed his new daughter-in-law, "Maybelle, I welcome you as a daughter and I sincerely hope my wife will also. I apologize for her. Please just give her time."

Days, weeks, and months passed. At 11:30 a.m. on November 8, 1918, Maybelle gave birth to a baby girl. Captain Andy beamed with happiness—at last, a girl child in the Nesbitt family! His 5-year-old son, Joseph, looked at the sleeping infant and immediately called her "his baby." But Andrew, Jr., totally unprepared for fatherhood, stared in wonderment upon his little daughter. His mother, who loved babies, found no place in her heart for this, her first grandchild. Both mother and child were to her alien enemies, despoilers of her son. Maybelle, with joy radiating from her eyes, cradled her child to her heart and loved it passionately. She chose the name Viola for her firstborn, but the captain insisted the baby be called Katrina in memory of his own little girl, who had been accidentally killed many years before. Both had their way. The child's birth certificate read "Katrina Viola Nesbitt."

Maybelle and her twin sister, Clarabelle, oldest daughters of the Cravatte family, had had considerable practice in child care because of their younger siblings. However, everything Maybelle did in tending her own baby or in assisting with the household chores met with her mother-in-law's disapproval. Junior, completely dominated by his mother, gave little support to his wife. After a few months, Captain Andy, sensing the friction and unhappiness in the home, helped the young couple establish a separate place of their own.

Although called "Captain," Mr. Nesbitt no longer followed the sea. Soon after Junior's birth, he had found a position as an engineer in the railroad yards where he worked until his death. However, the title "Captain" had stuck—it seemed to fit him.

Although he had been instrumental in getting the young couple to move to their own quarters, the captain missed them, especially the baby Katrina. Returning from work each evening, he would stop for a short visit with her and her parents. One day he noticed the baby showed signs of a cold—a runny nose, a slight fever. The next night the symptoms had worsened. The baby's throat seemed dry, a cough had developed, and the fever had shot up alarmingly. After a coughing spell, the poor child could hardly hold up her head. The young, inexperienced parents did not know what to do to help as they watched the little body wracked with coughing spells. Maybelle's younger sister and brothers had had colds but nothing like this.

When Grandpa came that evening and saw the condition of his cherished grandchild, he wrapped her in a blanket, and carefully holding her in one arm, jumped on his bike and pedaled as fast as he dared. Hurrying into his house, he called out, "Lois, hurry, call the doctor. I've brought Katrina home. The poor baby is ill."

A coughing spell shook the baby's body. Immediately Mrs. Nesbitt took the suffering child and watched as it tried to relieve its tortured lungs of excessive phlegm. The cough ended with a little whoop and a vomiting spell followed.

"Whooping cough," Lois asserted. Seeing how sick the baby had become, she could not refuse to try to nurse her back to health. However, she still resented the child's mother and could not resist flinging out, "Humph, the slut can't take care of her own brat!" But she called the family doctor, followed his instructions, and added things she had done for her boys when they had been afflicted with the "whoops." In 10 weeks Katrina fully recovered and should have been returned to her mother.

During all that time Maybelle had seen little of her infant because of the strained relations between herself and Miss Lois. Only when accompanied by the captain or her husband did she feel free to enter the senior Nesbitt's home. But now that her baby had recovered, Maybelle asked that the child be returned to her. All her pleas, however, fell on deaf ears. Captain Andy had become so attached to the baby that he did not want her to leave his home. While his wife disliked the child, she did not dare go against her husband's expressed wishes. Captain Andy, a loving, even indulgent husband, demanded little, but when he did, Lois knew he meant it.

Maybelle appealed to her husband. However, since he had not fully assumed his marital duties but depended largely upon his parents for support, he did not feel free to champion his wife's

ORIGINS

desires. In fact, Lois soon succeeded in separating the young couple. She sent Andrew to New York City to stay with her husband's brother, ostensibly to study tailoring. Bereaved of both husband and child, Maybelle returned to her own mother. Her sisters gathered around to comfort her while her grandmother Celeste sent up prayers for her and for Katrina, the great-grandchild she could not have to hold. At the same time she poured out imprecations upon all Britishers.

After countless attempts to get her child from the Nesbitts, Maybelle, with the help of her parents, took the case to court and sued for custody of her child. The judge ruled in her favor but stipulated that she should reimburse the senior Nesbitts fifty cents per day for the six years they had kept Katrina. Unable at that time to raise the required amount of money, Maybelle lost the case and the court awarded permanent custody to Andrew and Lois Nesbitt. They immediately adopted Katrina legally, making her joint heir with their sons.

3

THE EARLY YEARS

Katrina remembers only snatches of her first few years in her grandparents' home. When Papa brought her home during the whooping-cough incident, he had her crib moved into his room so that he could watch over and care for her during the night. Evidently the crib remained there for some time, for Katrina remembers her grandfather wakening her in the early morning to share his breakfast hour before he went to work. He enjoyed listening to her prattle and watching her enjoy her food.

Home in the evening, he hugged and kissed her, held her in his lap, and spoke words of tenderness and love, giving her a sense of security and love. As soon as she could toddle, she followed him everywhere. Whenever possible he took her with him. Sometimes he would stop by the Cravattes and let her spend some time with her real mother who would then lavish her love upon her child. While Katrina recognized the sincerity of her mother's love and treasured it, the thralldom of her grandfather's more frequent and continuous demonstrations of affection made a stronger bond between him and the girl.

Mama Lois, forced to take care of the unwanted grandchild, did all the proper things mechanically—no hugs, kisses, or tender words. Appearances and social position meant much to her. Although her son by his marriage had let the family down socially, she must bring his daughter up as befitted a proper Britisher. Accordingly Lois dressed Katrina in the best that she could obtain from the most prestigious stores in Miami. She provided new things for each season, for every holiday, and for various church and school functions. Mrs. Nesbitt held several prominent positions in her church, and she saw to it that the Nesbitt daughter represented the family status admirably.

But none of this finery brought Katrina happiness. The lack

THE EARLY YEARS

of love, totally missing in Lois's heart, made the clothes a burden rather than a joy. As she grew older the girl would give away her clothes to any child who asked for them or who looked as though she needed a dress, a pair of shoes, or anything else Katrina might be wearing. She seemed to have an inbred sense of caring. On one occasion she came home without her socks and new pair of patent leather pumps. Mama Lois had gone out and was thus not at home when the girl returned. Her grandfather saw the barefoot girl and asked, "Where are your shoes and socks? Did those new pumps hurt your feet?"

"No, Papa, I gave them to a little girl who had none. I have lots of shoes and socks," she replied happily as she wriggled her toes.

"So you do, so you do. And you've a heart big enough for the world. But go now and put on some shoes before Mama comes back and scolds."

Not only did she treat her clothes lightly, but she also treated expensive accessories with indifference. Parasols made excellent sticks for hitting tin cans found on the walk or in the gutters, beautiful leghorn hats could be taken off and forgotten. One could tire of swinging a little pocketbook, and after it had been properly admired and its contents noted, it could be given away. With Papa home, Mama Lois would only scold and call her a no-good, ungrateful commoner. But when her good clothes and expensive accessories disappeared and Papa was not around to defend her, Mama Lois not only shouted at her, but also slapped her hard several times until her ears rang. To the tingling of face and ears would come the words "You little—, you don't appreciate anything." *Why,* the girl wondered, *did Mama consider her bad because she gave her things away? Papa didn't think so.*

In spite of her grandmother's punishments and unkind words, Katrina thrived and grew strong. Soon able to play with her 5-year-older uncle Joseph, she became his defender. Chubby little "Joe" had a hard time protecting himself when playmates took his toys, chased, or fought him. At an early age Katrina showed her natural tendency to champion the hurting and fought her young uncle's battles.

KATRINA STANDS ALONE

Captain Andy provided abundantly for his family. He ordered staples in large quantities, and much fruit came from the varied trees he had planted on the property. The family purchased other fruits and vegetables as desired. Papa even had a section of garden where he raised his special Friday evening treat—fresh roasted peanuts. Katrina delighted in joining him. In fact, like her uncles, she had an excellent appetite. In addition to her early breakfast with Papa, she also joined Mama and the boys for the regular meal. Her uncles ate rapidly, Katrina slowly. Mrs. Nesbitt expected her to be through eating at the same time her sons were. With her husband not at home, she would rush the girl from the table and her unfinished meal. Then she would scrape the remaining food into the garbage or give it to the dog. Katrina learned not to cry for fear of boxed ears but to wait patiently for the next meal to appease her hunger. However, her lower lip would drop as she watched her unfinished sweet potato or green beans or dessert, if she had any, disappear from the table. If she asked for a between-meal orange, Mama usually sucked out most of the juice before giving the fruit to her grandchild. Later on when she learned to climb trees, she could pick and enjoy an orange and other fruit growing in the yard.

Unless Papa sat at the head of the table, Katrina had to watch her uncles devour chicken breasts or drumsticks with relish while she gnawed away on necks, backs, and an occasional wing. But with her grandfather present, he saw to it that only choice pieces found their way to Katrina's plate. Mama Lois would frown and in a disapproving voice say, "Andy, you spoil that girl to death!" He would laugh and Katrina, eyes twinkling, would glance up, her mouth full, her feet swinging happily.

A typical "little sister," as she grew old enough she played with all her uncles—running, jumping, laughing as they did. She joined them in topspinning and marbles, in fence and tree climbing, in their games of baseball and stickball. Also she took part in their fisticuffs and learned to handle a gun and shoot at a target. In quieter moments she watched her uncles wash, fix, and drive their cars. A keen observer of the mechanics of driving, Katrina learned to drive without lessons.

Boys usually love to tease little sisters, and her uncles were no exception. But most of the time they balanced their harassment with good care and affection for the youngest member of their family—all except Uncle Theodore. Quick-tempered and fond of giving orders, unless restrained by one of his brothers, he would frequently hit Katrina over the head if she did not follow some demand of his instantly. Mama Lois never scolded or punished him for this even when the hitting was done in her presence. Not until when in her early teens Katrina threateningly picked up an ax did he stop such behavior. However, in their adult years Theodore and Katrina developed a delightful relationship.

Her uncles had one activity that Katrina watched but would not attempt—ocean swimming. She feared the rolling waves. One day while at the beach her uncles decided the time had come for her to swim. They picked her up bodily and threw her out far from shore. Realizing that she had to either swim or sink, she began moving her arms and legs as she had seen swimmers do and made it to shore under the watchful eyes of her laughing uncles. A wave had knocked her down, she had swallowed sea water, her eyes stung from the salt, and her newly washed hair, long and thick, seemed to hold half the ocean. After sputtering her displeasure, Katrina refused to speak to her uncles for the rest of the day. But she could swim—a little.

Mrs. Nesbitt's sister Rachel came to live in Miami. A teacher and well-known disciplinarian in a girls' correction school in Nassau, she opened a school for kindergartners in her Miami home. Katrina became one of her great-aunt's pupils, learning rapidly and well. Even today she recalls memorizing the alphabet as taught to British children. One evening she sat on Papa's lap and flawlessly repeated the letters in their proper order. Her grandfather praised her highly.

But one day she experienced Aunt Rachel's displeasure. The annoyed teacher yanked her from her seat, whipped up her dress, pulled down her panties, and gave her several hard whacks on her bottom. The punishment not only hurt but also embarrassed the child. When at home she told her woes to Mama, she received no sympathy. Later when Papa asked his usual question about her day and learned of his little granddaughter's humiliating experience, he uttered an ultimatum: "Never again will you return to Aunt Rachel's school!" Then he added, "I don't believe in spanking little girls. There is no place on their bodies to hit them. You can't strike them in the face or head and spoil their looks, possibly their senses. And their bodies are for bearing children. You can't harm or destroy the most precious bodies in the world. You just can't hit a girl child!"

During his little tirade, Katrina lay cuddled up in his arms, fully agreeing with all he said.

But Mr. Nesbitt was not finished. "Lois," he ordered, "get this child ready to enter the church school the boys attend. When is registration day?"

His wife tossed her head angrily. "All this fuss over a little spanking! As stubborn as that little brat is, Rachel probably didn't give her enough stripes! I'm planning to send her to our church school since she is now old enough. Registration is Monday week. I'll have her ready."

"Good," he replied as he walked away with the child trotting behind him.

Soon a row of new dresses with matching bloomerlike panties hung in Katrina's closet. On opening day Mrs. Nesbitt dressed her granddaughter in a set made from the finest cotton. A ribbon on her combed and well-brushed hair and new socks and shoes completed the girl's first day's outfit. Mama Lois thought her child's attire perfect. So did Katrina as she bounced along the way with her uncles, a happy smile telling the world, "Look, I'm a big girl now. I'm going to real school."

But alas, when she entered the classroom, the children already present began to snicker, except one little girl. She had already been laughed at because her panties, like Katrina's, hung down below her dress British style. Cheeks flushed, teeth clenched, Katrina took the seat the teacher assigned her. She pulled up the offending bloomers above her knees. Mama and Aunt Rachel might favor the British style of dress for little girls, but they didn't attend an American school.

4

THROUGH THE GRADES

The teacher gently scolded the children, making them feel ashamed and apologetic for their rudeness. Katrina liked Miss Reid. She hadn't realized that the nice lady who had recently come to room in Papa and Mama's house would really be her teacher.

Miss Celeste Reid, first-grade teacher of the Bethany parochial school, contrasted sharply with Aunt Rachel. Miss Reid spoke softly, smiled a lot, even laughed with her pupils. She made her small charges feel smart and important as she worked with them at their individual levels. Katrina and her classmates responded by trusting, loving, and wanting to please their teacher. Katrina adored her and eventually they became lifelong friends.

Other grades and other teachers followed, some good, some not so good as Katrina remembers them. Mama Lois watched her progress, but instead of encouraging her grandchild to do well, constantly prophesied she'd be nothing more than a slovenly, promiscuous person. So deeply did Lois convince herself that her son's 15-year-old bride's French island ancestry made her a strumpet that she could not accept her as a member of the Nesbitt family nor could she accept Maybelle's child. However, in spite of her feelings, she, at her husband's insistence and approval, provided the girl with opportunities for growth and development. When Katrina reached the age of 8 or 9, Mama hired a capable voice and piano teacher for her grandchild. Katrina had an excellent ear for music and perfect pitch, and she enjoyed music lessons. She soon learned to play hymns and classical music. Mama Lois delighted in showing her off at church and other functions. In Mama's absence Katrina played by ear the songs and popular music of her day to the delight of her peers.

KATRINA STANDS ALONE

No schoolmates laughed at her now. Fun-loving, kind, generous, and a defender of the weak, she drew the other children to her. School for her became a happy place until a teacher's thoughtless discipline evoked the worst in Katrina. Miss Lillie Emmanuel, although well versed in subject matter, knew little about discipline with love. Sixth-graders need love as much as first-graders do, and Miss Emmanuel taught sixth grade.

Because she felt unwelcome in the Nesbitt home, Maybelle would occasionally visit Katrina at her school during the noon recess. One day she brought a special gift for her firstborn, a pretty lavaliere. She placed it around her daughter's neck, kissed her, and left immediately. When Miss Emmanuel had the children line up to go back into their classroom, she saw the necklace. With a vicious jerk she yanked it from the girl's neck, breaking the clasp. At her command the children filed into the room and took their seats, all except Katrina who stood by her desk, waiting. The teacher closed the door, walked briskly to her desk in the front of the room, then placed the lavaliere on her desktop. Katrina walked up to the teacher's desk.

"Well, why are you standing here?" the teacher demanded.

"Miss Emmanuel, please give me my necklace," Katrina asked softly, yet pleadingly.

"No, you had no business with it around your neck."

"But, Miss Emmanuel, my mother just gave it to me. She put it around my neck."

"No matter. You know the rules; No heathen baubles in this school! Let your adorning be a meek and quiet spirit. Take your seat."

Feeling anything but meek and quiet, Katrina stretched out her arm to pick up the lavaliere. As she did so, the woman picked up a wire coat hanger from the desktop and raked the girl's outstretched arm with its sharp end, causing a trickle of blood. Katrina winced with pain as she withdrew her arm.

"I said, take your seat. You'll not wear any heathen baubles and trinkets in this school. I don't care where you get them."

Grieved by the loss of her mother's gift and furious with her teacher, the girl walked reluctantly back to her seat, lower lip extended and fire in her eyes. Too angry to cry, she sat, body tense. She remained courteous but took no part in the ongoing lessons the remainder of that day, not even her favorite subject, social studies. To all questions she answered, "I don't know," her mind too busy struggling with unanswerable questions. Why did her teacher get so upset over her mother's gift? Did she feel the same way about Maybelle as Mama Lois did? Katrina knew her father and mother were married.

During one of Katrina's visits to the Cravattes, Maybelle had shown her the marriage certificate. It had her father's name, Andrew Nesbitt, Jr., on it as well as that of Maybelle Cravatte. She also knew she had two younger sisters. Were they called those awful names Mama had called her and Maybelle? Why could they stay with their mother while she had to remain with her grandmother? Would she really become all those bad things Mama said she would? She walked home alone that afternoon, trying to steel herself against whatever evil forces could cause her downfall.

Arriving home, she decided she did not need to tell Mama about the necklace. Her grandmother would only rant and rage when she found out Maybelle had given it to her. There would be all those awful names again, too. Mama would blame her for enticing her mother to the school behind her back. That could rate a beating. And besides, Mama liked Miss Emmanuel and thought she could do no wrong. Katrina decided to put some iodine on the deep scratch on her arm and as much as possible keep her sleeves down. She hoped Miss Emmanuel would say nothing about the incident. Fortunately for Katrina, she didn't.

In Bethany, as in many other parochial schools, parents bought all their children's textbooks and school supplies. At the beginning of the school year, Lois made certain all her children, including Katrina, had everything required. Some other children were less fortunate. When a classmate had no textbook, Katrina generously shared hers. Weeks after the necklace episode Katrina finished an assignment from one of her books and passed it across the aisle to a girl who had no book. Then she put her elbows on her desk and buried her head in her hands. Miss Emmanuel saw the transfer and accused Katrina of talking.

KATRINA STANDS ALONE

"I was not talking, Miss Emmanuel," the girl assured her teacher.

"You were talking," Miss Emmanuel asserted.

"I was not!" Katrina declared positively but still politely.

"*I* said you were talking," the teacher shouted, getting the complete attention of the entire class.

"I was *not* talking," came the definite answer.

Strap in hand, Miss Emmanuel walked menacingly up the aisle to Katrina's desk. "I said you were talking," she hissed, eyes narrowed in anger.

Again Katrina denied the charge. Her palms began to sweat, her brows drew together, she bit her lower lip, her body tensed like a coiled spring. The teacher lashed out at her, hitting her on her back and shoulders. Katrina sprang up like a jack-in-the-box, grabbed the strap, and forced her teacher against the rear wall where she banged her head against the chalkboard repeatedly. Her tussles with her uncles had made her as strong as any boy her size and also taught her the best holds. It took several of the larger boys in the class to free the teacher. Shaking off her restrainers, Katrina went back to her seat, still breathing hard, fists clenched. She felt hurt that her teacher would not believe her, and angry at the unwarranted punishment. Miss Emmanuel composed herself, regained control of the class, and went on with the day's activities. A special stillness hovered over the room. To her classmates Katrina had become a kind of heroine.

Although she expected to be severely punished, Katrina's anger, strong enough to give her courage, enabled her to tell Mama Lois what had happened. Instead of the expected blows or even harsh words, Mrs. Nesbitt chuckled and said, "That Lillie!" Katrina's eyes widened. Would she ever understand Mama, she wondered as she turned and walked away in amazement. To herself she thought, *I fought with my teacher, one of Mama's friends, and she only laughed. Could Mama be sick or something?* The whole experience so buoyed up her sense of worth that when Papa asked about her school day, she smiled and arms akimbo answered happily, "Just fine, Papa. Just fine!" Days later when Miss Emmanuel came to visit Mama, Katrina, listening from the next room, heard her grandmother say,

THROUGH THE GRADES

"Lillie, never use a strap on Katrina. If she says she didn't do something, believe her. The girl doesn't lie."

Mama defending me? Could it be she cares about me a little? Such thoughts puzzled her for a long time. The harsh discipline at home and sometimes at school constantly troubled her. Her primary source of security, of being wanted, of being loved, came from Papa, and now he, too, would leave her. While at work in the railroad yards the year Katrina had problems with her sixth-grade teacher, a fellow engineer ran his locomotive over Mr. Nesbitt, injuring him severely. Although they rushed him to the hospital, he died two days later. Katrina now found herself completely at the mercy of his wife.

People came from Jacksonville, Tampa, St. Petersburg; from New Jersey and New York; from Nassau, Jamaica, and the Virgin Islands, as well as from Miami and nearby Deerfield, to attend the funeral. Both Black and White honored Captain Andy, a well-respected and a well-loved man. But none, not even his wife, grieved as did Katrina. Her sorrow, too deep for tears, nearly broke her heart. She had lost her Papa, the only one who consistently showed his love for her. Her protector, her guide, her everything, had gone! How could she live without him?

Then an old friend, Zelma Hodge, a teacher who had been staying in the Nesbitt home at the time of Katrina's birth, came to join the mourners and comfort the family. She gave the girl the loving consolation she so desperately needed. The emotional floodgates opened and healing tears flowed. Somehow Katrina believed life could go on.

About a year before the accident, Captain Andy had made his decision for Christ and joined his wife and family as a member of the Bethany church. He had always believed its doctrines and had generously supported it financially but had hesitated to make a personal commitment. His decision for Christ and his accidental death made a profound influence upon Katrina. She had attended church since infancy, but now she would give her heart, herself, to Jesus as her grandfather had done, and in so doing she gained a wonderful relationship with the Supreme Lover of humanity. With even greater fervor than that with which she had followed Papa, she now walked reverently with her Lord.

KATRINA STANDS ALONE

Like all little girls of her day, Katrina had to perform simple household chores. However, she had the good fortune of not being overburdened with heavy tasks as long as her grandfather lived. He saw to it that Lois hired help to do most of the heavy cleaning and laundering. With a large house and sometimes five boys to raise; with the house a mecca for church dignitaries and workers and Mama as hostess, Papa gladly paid for help. For a long time this relieved Katrina of too much arduous work, but not from Mrs. Nesbitt's impatience. Slow-moving and methodical, the girl irked her grandmother, who moved effortlessly and quickly. A request to bring her sewing basket would send Katrina scurrying off for it, but instead of returning quickly and gracefully with it, she would come shuffling along, fearful that she might spill the contents and arouse the woman's ire. Mama would then scold, "Pick up your feet, you lazy slut," and in trying to hurry, Katrina might spill half the basket's contents. It would call forth other unsavory name-callings and a well-aimed kick as the girl tried to pick up the dropped contents. The girl became afraid to go near her grandmother because she never knew when the woman would hit her.

Setting and clearing the table and washing dishes were early tasks allotted to Katrina. However, if she did not fold the napkins to Mama's liking, place the silver properly, or fill the water glasses just so, Katrina would feel the sting of Mama's hand or fist on the top of her head or against her ear. No explanation followed. It became a guessing game in which, unless she made the right conclusion, more blows would follow. It happened so often that even when she made no mistakes, she shrank away whenever Mama Lois approached her.

A good housekeeper, Mrs. Nesbitt expected perfection on a new skill on the first try. Her impatience made her a poor teacher. Even her presence intimidated Katrina, making her forget instructions and sequences on varied tasks. On the other hand, and for some unknown reason, Mama, an excellent cook, allowed the girl to watch and even help in food preparation and cooking. As a result, Katrina rapidly learned to enjoy the culinary arts and later in high school chose them as her major.

Mama also did beautiful embroidery and crochet work. She

THROUGH THE GRADES

taught her granddaughter the basic stitches and bought materials and patterns for her so Katrina could practice. However, Mama would not show her how to correct mistakes. The girl had to figure them out for herself. Nor would the grandmother give satisfactory answers to questions. Generally her reply would be, "Stupid, are you so dumb you don't know that?" Katrina would turn away, feeling abashed and thinking that maybe she was stupid. On the other hand, her grandmother would buy books and leave them where Katrina could find them. An avid reader, Katrina often found answers through such reading. But Mama's handling of questions in this manner made it difficult for the girl to ask other adults questions for fear she would get the same kind of response. Although she early learned the value of the dictionary, she missed mother-daughter talks that would have made things so much easier.

After accepting Christ, Katrina felt she should apologize to her teacher. She lingered one day after class to speak to her teacher. "Miss Emmanuel, I'm sorry I hurt you that day when I banged your head against the chalkboard. I was very, very angry when you insisted I had been talking. I guess it had to be pent-up anger, for I had not forgiven you for destroying the necklace my mother had put on my neck. I hadn't lied to you, and I hurt."

"I'm sorry too, Katrina. Knowing you as I do, I should have believed you. Yes, I freely forgive you."

"Thank you, Miss Emmanuel. I feel better. Now may I please have the necklace? I won't wear it. I only want to keep it, for I have so few things from my real mother."

"I'm sorry, 'Trina; it's gone. I threw it in the trash, knowing Mama Lois wouldn't let you wear it anyway."

"But I could have kept it to remind me of my mother."

"Well, I saw that necklace as the breaking of a rule and had I let you keep it, your classmates would think they could wear jewelry too. But now I see I should have believed you and let you take the bauble home. I'm really sorry for not believing and trusting you. You see, teachers sometimes make mistakes just like students do, because they do not think. Forgive me?"

A slow smile broke out on Katrina's face as she said, "Yes, Miss Emmanuel. I forgive you." With their differences settled,

KATRINA STANDS ALONE

the girl picked up her books and walked home.

In spite of an occasional unpleasant happening, school made an excellent haven. There the friendship of classmates and success in her lessons gave her belief in herself. She did not have to be any of those terrible things Mama said she would be. No, she'd study hard and make her grandmother proud of her. She entered the seventh grade determined to excel, but Mama increased her home duties, making life as difficult as possible. She did well but not as well as she had hoped.

In the eighth grade she found a kind, understanding teacher, Catherine Murray, who like Mrs. Hodge and the first-grade teacher, became a lifelong friend. Miss Murray knew Katrina's home life caused her much unhappiness. Thus she dealt with the girl in such a way that she trusted her and opened her heart to her teacher. Now she had someone with whom she could communicate, to whom she could go with questions and not be made to feel foolish and stupid. She did well in Miss Murray's class, and when graduation time came, she headed the list of graduates.

Katrina remembers the graduation with mixed emotions. The usual excitement reigned among the students. She describes the anticipation of the nine prospective graduates, herself included, as bubbly as a tall glass of Mama Lois's freshly brewed root beer. New white dresses, white socks, and slippers or pumps made up the girls' graduation attire. Mama had a beautiful white pongee dress made for Katrina, and she purchased pumps and all the necessary accessories from one of the most prestigious Miami stores. The Nesbitt daughter must shine before the public. However, since she had always worn the best, the clothes caused Katrina no special thrill.

All the graduates looked forward to having their parents, siblings, and as many relatives and friends as possible witness the greatest happening so far in their young lives. But graduation night conflicted with the opening of the annual Florida camp meeting. Would parents delay going to camp meeting just to see their sons and daughters graduate from grade school? Naturally the children expected them to. Katrina wondered if Mama would stay. How she hoped she would! The girl had worked so hard to make her grandmother proud of her. But for Mama no choice

THROUGH THE GRADES

remained—camp meeting came first. She had made all the preparations for Katrina's graduation. Mary, her son Joseph's young wife, could supervise and see that the girl dressed properly and that she made it on time for the exercises. Lois Nesbitt had to be at the camp meeting miles away.

Beautifully dressed but sadly disappointed, Katrina sat among the graduates, her brown eyes glistening with unshed tears, lips unsmiling as she faced a sea of cheerful faces. In her heart she cried out, *I so much wanted Mama to see me graduate and be proud of me. Perhaps then she could love me.*

Others were there who did care for her—Joseph and Mary; Ella, a family friend whom she liked very much; and, of course, her teacher, Miss Murray. Katrina blinked, a single fat tear plopped into her lap. Vigorously shaking her head, she fought for control. Then their eyes met and smiles broke out on both their faces. Maybelle, Katrina's real mother, had come to see her graduate from her first milestone on the road of education. Katrina's recently brooding eyes now sparkled like sun-drenched water and she wriggled with happiness. She had longed for Mama and had been given a greater joy, her real mother. Now she, Katrina Viola Nesbitt, would perform her part on the program perfectly. Everyone present would be proud of her.

They did not speak to each other. Maybelle left as soon as the diplomas had been given to the graduates. She would not cause her child embarrassment nor a scolding from Miss Lois. But by her presence the message came through, "I love you, my darling, I love you."

5

TEENAGE ABUSE

Soon after Captain Andy's death, his wife began dismissing household help and placing more and more tasks upon her 12-year-old grandchild. Katrina's tasks began with the early morning, washing the large kitchen floor. Mornings in Miami could be cold. Being aroused at five o'clock to do the scrubbing on one's knees didn't rate as the most pleasant way to start the day, especially when the water had not had time to become hot and the tiles had to be rubbed until they glistened, all corners and baseboards made immaculate, and every piece of movable furniture removed—not cleaned around or under—then carefully replaced.

When Mama came to stand in the doorway, her keen gray eyes would miss nothing. After feeling the impact of Mama's shoe, aimed with perfect accuracy at her head or bent back, Katrina might hear, "What is that chair doing over there?" She would wince at the blow, but if she tried to explain, another shoe might come with the words "Shut up, you lazy slut. You can't do anything right!" Upon hearing her grandmother's receding footsteps, Katrina's silent tears would mix with the scrub water.

Much of the cleaning fell on her young shoulders, and she had to do most of it before she could leave for school. She would hurriedly clean a room and go on to the next when she'd feel a hard slap across the side of her head. Not receiving any explanation, she would have to figure out what she had done wrong or had not done at all. With her ear burning from the slap, Katrina would go back and check her work, hoping desperately to find the cause of Mama's displeasure. If she failed, she would get another slap or blow, often for some little thing such as a picture slightly awry on the wall, a doily not quite centered. Large or small, each mistake received equal punishment. Nor did an alarm

TEENAGE ABUSE

clock awaken her for her tasks. Unless she spontaneously got up on time, she would receive a smack on her back or head. Mama became adept, too, at throwing things—shoes, slippers, anything. Other times she lashed out with one of her sons' belts or any kind of strap available. Katrina, as well as her uncles, got considerable practice in dodging. In time she swerved away every time Mama came near her. The habit led her later, even in college, to automatically dodge whenever any authority person approached her. The blows to the side of her head partially deafened one ear. However, the stern discipline made her an excellent housekeeper.

The long summer vacation following Katrina's eighth-grade graduation made little difference. She still had to get up at five in the morning. To the chores already a part of her day, Mama added laundering for the large family. The washing she had to do outdoors by hand in water warmed by the sun. She rinsed the clothes three or four times with water hosed out from the kitchen or yard faucet. If Mama found a piece not washed to her liking, she would wordlessly slap Katrina with it. She never said, "Here's a spot you didn't get," "Wash this over, it isn't clean," or even "Wash that shirt over. See that ring on the collar? You can do better than that."

The constant tension eased only when she had all the clothes hanging on the lines to dry and all washing paraphernalia carefully cleaned and properly put away. When that task was finished and the house was in perfect order, Mama would permit her to visit cousins or approved schoolmates, or she could spend the afternoon quietly at home. Often she stayed home those long afternoons. Usually little verbal communication took place between her and her grandmother. Each might silently sit in view of the other, crocheting, embroidering, or just reading. At such times Katrina longed for Mama to talk to her. But Mrs. Nesbitt's generally hostile attitude made it difficult for the girl to initiate a conversation, certainly not to ask a question.

Books helped greatly, but they also raised questions. Sometimes Katrina would find a comfortable crotch in one of the backyard trees, and there sheltered from view she would read, think, and brood. Often she wondered why certain things

KATRINA STANDS ALONE

happened—Why did Papa have to die? How could she get Mama to love her? Why didn't her real father come and take her so she could be with her two younger sisters? Why could they not all be together like in the stories she had been reading?

In mid-July of that summer Mama decided to visit relatives in New York City and take Katrina with her. They stayed several weeks. The girl had a wonderful time roaming about the streets, parks, and interesting places with her city cousins while her grandmother visited with the adults. However, all good things come to an end. The time came to return to Miami and high school.

6

ON TO HIGH SCHOOL

For the first time Katrina registered in a public school: Booker T. Washington High, a college preparatory school for Blacks. It had an excellent reputation for its course offerings, its teachers, and its graduates. However, transferring from a small, close-knit private school to one housed in such an imposing building and attended by hundreds of teenagers frightened yet challenged her. Attending Booker T. Washington High became an adventure into the future.

A widely diversified curriculum offered all the standard high school courses and more, making it possible to pursue many different fields. The faculty advised each student to choose a major field during his freshman year. Katrina chose home economics. She had enjoyed cooking at home. It had been the only household task Mama had let her do without harassment. Thus she had learned to take pleasure in preparing meals for that large family. Now perhaps she would learn to be a dietitian. Little did she realize that home economics also included dressmaking and tailoring, skills that held little appeal for her at that time. However, they would play a valuable part later in her life.

She entered wholeheartedly into the entire high school program. History and geography intrigued her. The parochial school lessons in those subjects had whetted her appetite for social studies. Science opened many new vistas, answered and raised so many questions. She reveled in the beauties of literature and began experimenting with poetry writing. So much to learn! So many new associations to make!

A little over two months into her freshman year, catastrophe struck. Her uncle Joseph, married and working in a mortuary, often accompanied his employer on trips to the hospital to pick up bodies. Idling at the desk of the County Hospital one day, he saw to his surprise the name Maybelle Bains listed in the register. He knew about his brother's divorce from Maybelle and her remarriage to Herman Bains, but he had not heard of her illness. Noting her room number, he went to see her. His former sister-in-law lay there, her luminous eyes lusterless, her body extremely frail. She recognized him and in a weak voice answered his questions, then begged him to ask Mrs. Nesbitt to let Katrina visit her. She wanted desperately to see her firstborn daughter once more before she died.

Deeply touched, Joe promised to ask his mother. True to his word, he hastened to tell Lois of Maybelle's condition and of her urgent request to see Katrina. The next day Mama Lois took the girl to the hospital to visit her mother. As they knocked and entered the room, Maybelle turned her lusterless eyes in their direction. Recognition dawned. Too weak to rise up in bed, she stretched out her arms and whispered, "Viola!"

Katrina Viola rushed over to her mother, and their tears mingled as they embraced. Mama Lois stood there, straight and tall, with a disapproving frown on her forehead. "Don't smother your mother," she called.

"Miss Lois, thanks so much for bringing Viola to see me. Won't you please sit down," Maybelle offered as Katrina drew away.

Mrs. Nesbitt sat gingerly on a straight chair as she asked Maybelle how she had become so ill.

In a rasping voice Maybelle asked, "Do you remember the tornado we had a while back?"

"Yes, I do," the older woman replied, wondering what that had to do with her illness.

"Well, it tore the roof off our house that night and the floodwaters poured in. My new baby and I were holed up in that wreck for two days before we were found. The baby died, and I got a bad fever and a cold. I took regular cold remedies, but they didn't do much good. I got worse."

"Where were your two girls and the baby's father during all this?"

"The girls were over at my mother's for the weekend. My husband, Herman Bains, is a Navy man, Miss Lois. His ship, out

ON TO HIGH SCHOOL

there on maneuvers, didn't pull in until a week later. By that time I'd been rescued but remained sick."

"Humph!" Mama Lois commented. "That tornado caused plenty of damage to a lot of people."

Katrina wanted desperately to do something to help restore her mother to health. If only her grandmother would let her take her mother home to their comfortable house, she, Katrina Viola, would be entirely responsible for her care and comfort. She would make rich, healing broths for her, feed her the best of foods to strengthen her, get the very best doctor, and see that she took his medicines—anything—if only. . . . But one look at Mama's stern face instantly told her what the answer would be.

Maybelle reached under her pillow and brought out a small chamois bag tied with a piece of white thread. As she handed the bag to Katrina she murmured, "This is for you. I know you don't wear jewelry, but keep this little token in remembrance of me. I've kept it a long time. I had hoped to give it to you to celebrate your sixteenth birthday, but I doubt I'll live to see that. On your sixteenth birthday take this ring out and let it tell you how very much I've always loved you. And when you grow up and have a little girl, be sure to tell her how much her grandmother would have loved her. But she couldn't wait to see her."

Tearfully Katrina answered, "Thank you, Mother. I'll keep it forever and I'll never, never forget you!" She opened the little bag to reveal a ring of gold with her birthstone, the topaz, encircled with tiny diamonds. Katrina could hardly believe her eyes. "It's beautiful! Thank you again, Mother. Oh! I'll keep this ring forever and ever. Look, Mama, isn't it beautiful?"

"Yes it is." Then quietly but firmly Mrs. Nesbitt continued, "I'll take it; you might lose it."

Obediently Katrina handed the ring and bag over to her grandmother, never to see them again. Years later when she asked for the ring, Mama told her she had forgotten what she had done with it.

At the hospital Mama Lois placed the ring in the little chamois bag, tied it with the thread, then put it in her handbag. "Come now, let's go. You've tired your mother."

"Yes, Mama." Katrina bent over and kissed Maybelle's

KATRINA STANDS ALONE

gaunt cheek and wordlessly followed her grandmother out of the room.

At home that evening, Joe and his wife, Mary; Andy, Jr., and his wife, Jessie Lee; and Mama had all gathered in the living room. Katrina stood by the newel post in the hall, her heart heavy with the premonition that she would never again see her mother alive. Silent tears streamed down her cheeks until with a deep sigh she threw her arms around the post and burst into heartbreaking sobs. Mama came into the hall and began slapping the young teenager over and over, saying "Stop that bleating—that slut never did anything for you."

The men jumped up, shocked at their mother's behavior. Mary ran to Katrina's aid, exclaiming, "Mama Lois, Mama Lois, stop hitting that girl like that!"

Jessie Lee, aghast at such shocking cruelty, joined Mary. Mama Lois glared at them, shook her head as if to free it from her fury, then with ramrod back and high head walked wordlessly down the hall. Katrina ran upstairs and locked herself in the bathroom. During the entire episode, Katrina's father, Andy, Jr., also home on a visit, stood on the front porch where he saw and heard his daughter's sobs and his mother's reaction, yet neither said nor did anything about it. He still couldn't brave his mother's wrath. Instead he left the porch and went into the wood house, maybe to weep himself.

Later Mary succeeded in getting Katrina to open the bathroom door, and in love comforted her. Maybelle died that night.

As soon as she learned of the death, Mama Lois magnanimously made funeral arrangements for Maybelle with her mortician. The Cravattes were deeply grateful and assumed that the breach between the two families had healed. Grandma Celeste Cravatte busied herself making a smocked shroud for her granddaughter's burial. Mama Lois bought a beautiful white dress for Katrina to wear to the funeral. The ceremony would be held on Sunday. After the Saturday morning service at Bethany and the family dinner, Mama permitted Katrina, in the company of her eighth-grade teacher, Miss Murray, to go to the funeral home to view her mother's body. Imagine their surprise when they learned that Maybelle Nesbitt-Bains had already been

ON TO HIGH SCHOOL

interred in Potters' Field by order of one Mrs. Lois Nesbitt. Katrina and her teacher were both stunned.

"Miss Murray," Katrina whispered as they walked away, "how could Mama do this to my mother? The Cravattes would have found a way to bury her had they known. They wouldn't have let her be buried in Potters' Field like a pauper!"

"I don't know why, 'Trina; I guess Miss Lois must have had a good reason."

"She lied! She didn't mean to help," Katrina declared. "If Papa had been alive, he wouldn't have allowed this to happen!"

"I know, 'Trina, this hurts. It hurts me, too. Your mother always impressed me by her gentleness and kindness and the constancy of her love for you. Maybe Mama Lois couldn't see these things. We mustn't judge. Let's go back to the church as planned and ask her why."

When Mama saw them come in, her expression did not change. After they told her what had happened, she replied, "Yes, I know," her gray eyes inscrutable.

"Why?" Katrina and Miss Murray asked together.

"She's where she belongs," the older woman answered as she tossed her head and walked away.

Katrina trembled with suppressed anger and hurt. Miss Murray's encircling arm drew her close as she comforted, "There, there, you'll understand someday. Remember, Jesus cares."

"Yes, Miss Murray," the girl answered, but to herself she thought, *It isn't fair. Mama makes it so hard to love her.*

The Cravattes had not been notified of the change. Maybelle never wore Grandmother Celeste's beautifully smocked shroud. The body had already been removed when the Cravattes arrived late Friday afternoon.

After Katrina's uncles and their wives had left for their own homes, she could speak of her grief to no one. She had to bottle it up inside herself. On Monday she returned to school as if all in her world went well. She found an outlet for her pent-up feelings by participating in the drama club. And the accuracy of her clear alto voice gave her entry into the Girls' Glee Club in which she sang for several years. True, she had to perform all her household tasks before leaving for her first class in the morning in order to gain after-school rehearsal time. But it was wonderful to lose oneself in group singing and acting.

Her home economics teacher, a rotund woman, noted for her culinary expertise, demanded perfection from her students. But if someone made a mistake, she would encourage the student to try again. Under Mrs. Sanders' tutelage, Katrina became an excellent cook. A mutual liking existed between them. Often when invited to present a cooking demonstration at the nearby White high school, Mrs. Sanders would take Katrina along as her assistant and allow her to make it. Katrina became quite famous for her cakes and received two awards.

Only one of Mrs. Sanders' rules bothered Katrina. Each student had to eat some of everything she/he cooked. "Sweet potato pie? Fine! But white potato pie? Ugh! Who ever heard of such a thing? No, thank you, no." Katrina usually found a way to avoid tasting the unknown or disliked. It is still hard to get her to try anything unusual or that she thinks she will not enjoy.

In her senior year two colleges offered her scholarships; Hampton Institute and Howard University. Her future looked good—that is if Mama Lois would trust her away from Miami.

In spite of her childhood, Katrina had become an affable, fun-loving teenager. She had an excellent ear for music and could play any of the popular songs once she heard them. Not at home, of course, with Mama around—then only hymns and classics. She and the church frowned on dancing, too. But Katrina soon picked up the current steps from her schoolmates. All one had to do was watch, and she had plenty of willing teachers.

Inevitably the male students became aware of her. Her good nature and willingness to help others plus her infectious laughter attracted both sexes. Boys were fine in a group, but she shied away from all male attention. Wasn't this, according to Mama, what made girls bad? If Mama was right, she reasoned, all boys made girls bad like her father had made her mother bad. Yet in her heart Katrina did not believe her mother had been like Mama Lois said she was. But all those awful names Mama called her. Katrina did not wish them to apply to her. Because her grand-

ON TO HIGH SCHOOL

mother made her fear all men, she would accept no male advances until . . .

The Davises—Fred, Viola, and Alphonso, all good friends of Mama's—lived in a pleasant home with a private beach in Miami Beach. Katrina and Alphonso—or Sonny Man as they called him—became friendly through the close association of the two families. Friendship grew into fondness, fondness into love—at least, for Sonny Man.

But what about Katrina? She enjoyed his company. It pleased her to have him take her places and to know that Mama trusted him. But he wanted to go steady, he talked of marriage and of settling down. Settling down! Katrina had been settled down all her life—now she wanted action. The time had come to break away. Sure, someday she hoped to marry, but not yet. She must first find herself. And Katrina avidly did exactly that. Mama had made her feel stupid, unworthy of love, and by inheritance and birth immoral. She needed time to prove to herself and to the world that she, as an intelligent, virtuous Christian woman, deserved the esteem, the trust, and the love of others. No, she knew that she was not yet ready for a lifetime commitment. She must have time to grow.

With set jaw she made up her mind. *I'm going to college, get a degree—something no other Nesbitt has ever done so far. True, Theo went to college for a while, but he did not finish. I, Katrina Viola Nesbitt, will finish something and be somebody. I'll try to become as good a home economics teacher as Mrs. Sanders and a good, kind, loving Christian, able to help others.*

Commencement night Katrina marched down the long aisle, determined and proud. This time Mama sat in the audience accompanied by her son Joseph, his wife Mary, and their 3-year-old son Junior. In her heart Mrs. Nesbitt must have been proud of the accomplishments of her first grandchild. All through her teens and high school days Katrina had brought no dishonor upon the Nesbitt name. As the graduates came down the aisle, at the sight of Katrina, her little nephew clapped his hands and shouted, "Lay 'em down, Aunt 'Trina, lay 'em down!"

7

AN ADVENTURE INTO FREEDOM

The four years in the Booker T. Washington High School of Miami had accomplished much for Katrina. Not only had they increased her knowledge, but they had also provided an excellent social outlet for her growth and assured her that, in spite of Mama's prophecies, she had it within herself to be a person of worth. She felt good about herself.

A few weeks later as Mrs. Nesbitt sat peacefully rocking on the front porch, Katrina broke the silence between them. "Mama, I would like to accept the Hampton Institute scholarship. It is an excellent opportunity—tuition for four full years. I could work for my board and room. Lots of girls do. May I?"

"What for?" the older woman asked. "So you can turn out to be a strumpet like your mother?"

That hurt. Katrina's cheeks burned. For the first time she stood up to her grandmother. "If I were going to be bad, to be the things you think my mother did, I would have done so long ago right here in Miami. There are plenty of opportunities!"

Although by this time the beatings had stopped, Mama still threw a shoe or slipper with deadly accuracy when crossed or angry. Katrina braced herself, but nothing came nor did the grandmother respond to the girl's tirade. However, several days later, out of a clear sky, Lois told her, "I don't like the idea of you going to that Hampton school. Why don't you go to Oakwood? Several of the girls from the church are going there. You'd be with people you know and not with strangers. Many of our best ministers and teachers trained at Oakwood College. It's a good school." After a brief pause she continued, "If you go there, I'll pay all your expenses."

AN ADVENTURE INTO FREEDOM

Katrina dropped her gaze. Having set her heart on Hampton Institute, the school of her home economics teacher whom she wished to emulate, she didn't want to go to Oakwood College. But now Mama had dashed all such hopes. Looking up, she said in a resigned voice, "Thank you, Mama. I'll go to Oakwood to please you."

Her grandmother smiled and nodded her head in satisfaction. Turning, Katrina left the room to brood over her disappointment. Mama had made a generous offer—to pay all her expenses, but it wouldn't buy what Katrina wanted. Oh, to be 18, or better yet 21, and free to do as she wished. Well, she reasoned, she would be going to a college. All had not been lost.

When several members of the Bethany church learned the Nesbitt girl would attend Oakwood, they immediately put their daughters, also ready for college, in her charge. Accordingly, on a September day in 1938, she and two other girls made the long train ride from the southeast coast of Florida to the hilly regions of northern Alabama. Accustomed to long train rides, Katrina knew what to do, but for her companions the extended trip provided a novel experience. They gazed out the window, talked, giggled, and shared the lunches their mothers had provided for them. They slept uncomfortably in their seats until they arrived in Chattanooga. There they changed to the soon-to-become-familiar Joe Wheeler, the only train running between Chattanooga and Huntsville, Alabama. After sitting in merciless heat for more than two hours in a less than comfortable Jim Crow half coach that passed through sun-baked, insipid scenery, it sounded good to hear the conductor call out, "Next Stop Huntsville, Huntsville!"

The school team met the train as it chugged into the station and soon the three girls and their luggage began the five-mile trek to the college campus. The scenery was quite different from what they were familiar with. No palm trees, no orange, avocado, guava, or other familiar fruit trees. A few blocks from the station the paved street gave way to a dirt road. And wonder of wonders, no sand but instead red earth. As they drove along, all they could see were a few seemingly isolated houses and field after field of cotton or corn.

KATRINA STANDS ALONE

At last the team pulled up between two large stone pillars that marked the entrance to Oakwood Junior College. Another dirt road flanked by a few frame houses led to a large, well-kept grassy circle, surrounded by college buildings and dormitories. They stopped at Irwin Hall, the main building for women and girls as both academy- and college-level students lived on different floors in the same building. The three weary travelers had reached their new home. After meeting their dean, they got settled in their assigned rooms, ready for registration the following day.

Katrina knew what she wanted. She would have to take other subjects, of course, but again her major would be home economics, this time with emphasis on dietetics. But alas, in 1938 Oakwood Junior College did not offer such a major. It had a few courses, but they duplicated those Katrina had already taken in high school. Her thwarted expectations did not warrant a return to Miami. However, she certainly did not wish to become either a minister or a Bible instructor. Nor did secretarial and business training interest her. While others milled about, getting their cards signed, Katrina sat scowling at the fate that had sent her to a school where she did not want to be and where she could not get what she wanted. With a deep sigh she got up, her mind made up. She would take the teacher-training course the registrar had suggested. *Mmm,* she mused, *if I become a teacher, later on I can get the rest of the home economics courses that I want. Then I'll be able to teach in a high school, just like Mrs. Sanders, or even in a college.*

Most of the classes interested her, and soon she fell into the routine of study. While she missed the camaraderie and activities of her high school years, she quickly made friends at Oakwood and enjoyed most of its pleasures, especially the long walks about the countryside. Something about the religious atmosphere at Oakwood appealed to her. It seemed to fit in with those eight years at the Bethany parochial school of her childhood. However, one element disturbed her—the Sabbath dress code for girls. Female attire from sunset Friday to sunset Saturday consisted of dark-blue skirts and starched white middy blouses. The blouses scratched and itched, making their wearers miserable. Along

AN ADVENTURE INTO FREEDOM

with nearly all the other girls and young women, Katrina fussed and complained about them until day's end. Then after vespers they'd rush to their rooms, take off the offending uniform, and dress as they wished. Katrina would sputter to her roommates and any girls nearby, "I've got all these lovely Sabbath dresses hanging in my closet and can't wear them. Why, oh why did I have to come here!"

It didn't take long for Katrina to discover why Mama felt Oakwood was a safe place for her to be. Not only was it a religious school; the coeducational aspect had plenty of limitations. In the classrooms the sexes could sit together, but in chapel and worship services they occupied different sides of the auditorium and church. The school followed the same practice for all concerts, lectures, etc. Walk days and going-into-town days alternated weekly by sexes. Only college-age young ladies could receive male visitors and then only by arrangement with the dean of women. When the young man arrived, the dean would call the young woman and the couple would have the privacy of one of the living rooms for a brief period of time. The administration would withhold the privilege if the young lady's conduct or grades were unsatisfactory.

During her two years at Oakwood Junior College, Katrina made many friends. In addition to roommates, they included four special ones: Mildred Strachan (Rogers), from Nassau; Mildred Evelyn (Jones), of Delaware; Katie M. Walker (Soughs), of Newport News, Virginia; and Julie Brown (Mattingly), of Charleston, South Carolina. The first three were working their way through school. Besides paying all her expenses Mama also sent Katrina large sums of spending money. Her own needs were so few she could easily help her three friends purchase necessities they often could not afford. During Katrina's second year, Julie Brown came to Oakwood and roomed with Mildred Evelyn. The four banded together like sisters and remain so to this day.

A number of Oakwood's faculty members had met Mama Lois. They had enjoyed her hospitality and knew she had money. Now they vied for Katrina's friendship. But the girl doubted their sincerity. Did they really want to befriend her, or did they wish to gain favor with her grandmother through her? Katrina kept her distance.

Near the beginning of her second year at Oakwood a woman from the North arrived, bringing new ideas about deaning in a dormitory of mixed academy and college young women. While supporting the deep religious and moral concepts of the school, she added cultural and recreational ideas that made life less like that of a convent. Katrina and her "sisters" were among those who appreciated the new program. They recognized in the new person someone who, as a Christian educator, had a true interest in them as individuals and could be trusted. One by one they accepted her as "Mommie" or "Mother," seeking her advice, asking for guidance. Nothing pleased them more than to sneak downstairs to her apartment for a conference after lights were out at 9:30. Admiring their dean, they wanted to get close to her. They sensed that she must have had a traumatic experience at some time that made her, at first, seem guarded, even closed.

If at all possible, they would one by one softly knock at their dean's door after she had made her rounds and seen that all her girls were in their rooms and bedded down. Then before presenting their problems or questions, they would turn down their dean's bed, wait for her to bathe and change, offer to massage her back and shoulders, and choose her dress and accessories for the next day (when she'd let them).

At first only Mildred Evelyn and Katrina came. Katie, who roomed directly over the dean's apartment, became jealous when she learned of the two young women's after-hour visits. Piqued, she would bang on the floor to let them know how unhappy she felt to be left out. Rather than scold, the dean sent Mildred to invite her to join her "sisters." When Julie came the second year, she wanted to know where her roommate, Mildred Evelyn, went after "lights out." The others decided to invite her to join them. Julie became the "baby" sister of the foursome. At the end of the first year both Mildred and Katie stayed on campus to work and build up a credit for their next year's schooling. Katrina decided to stay also with her new friends rather than go home to a summer with Mama.

The work supervisor assigned her to the kitchen crew under

AN ADVENTURE INTO FREEDOM

the summer matron, Mrs. Cunningham, affectionately known as "Mother dear." One day the matron took a part of the kitchen crew, including Katrina, to pick wild blackberries growing on a nearby hillside. All went well until a harmless black snake slithered by a bush where she happily picked and ate the berries. At the sight of the snake Katrina leaped up in the air screaming, threw her partially filled pail away, and ran over to one of the other pickers. The commotion over, she warily began picking again after retrieving her pail. Then someone yelled "snake!" Again she tossed her pail into the air.

"Now, now, young ladies," Mrs. Cunningham scolded, "the snake is just as afraid of you as you are of it. Come now and get these berries picked."

"Yes, Miss Cunningham," they chorused as they went back to work. Fearfully, not fully sure whether the woman's statement was fact or fiction, Katrina rejoined the crew. All were silently gathering berries when she glanced down and thought she saw something moving. Without waiting to see what it could be, she hurled her berries to the ground and headed for the road only to stop when she heard the matron call, "Miss Katrina!"

"Yes, ma'am," the wild-eyed girl politely replied.

"Miss Katrina, you'd better go back to the kitchen. Come, get your pail and go help with dinner."

Never again did they send her after anything that grew on bushes or vines. However, so aptly did she fit into the work of planning, preparing, and serving meals that it became one of her permanent tasks.

When the college president learned that Katrina had had a course in library science in high school, he asked her to assist the hard-pressed librarian, Onilda Taylor. Soon she learned that Miss Taylor suffered from a duodenal ulcer and needed a special diet. Had Mrs. Cunningham been permanent matron all through the year, the librarian's need would not have been a problem. But the regular matron lacked compassion for the librarian. Even when food that Miss Taylor could eat graced the serving counters, the woman in charge of the dining hall would deny it to her. Katrina watched it happen several times and became furious. Finally she told the matron, "If ever again I see you snatch anything away from Miss Taylor's tray, you'll answer to me." The matron wanted no rift between herself and Katrina who knew too much about the mismanagement of the culinary and dining departments. Since she had the freedom of the kitchen, Katrina began preparing special dishes for the librarian. Maybe she'd be a dietitian after all.

By summer's end Katrina and her "sisters" had built up sizable credits toward their next year's schooling. After a short break at home she returned to continue her studies. To the girls' regret someone else occupied the dean's apartment in their dorm. Their "mommie" now chaired the Education Department and lived across campus in East Hall. No more after-hours mother-daughter group conferences. However, the relationship continued, and each girl found a way to get over to East Hall. The counseling continued, and they received the help they needed as did others.

Katrina's second year went well. She studied hard, received excellent grades, continued to work a few hours each day, and also found time for fun and recreation. On a May day in 1940 she graduated from Oakwood Junior College as a teacher.

8

TEACHER GOES TO THE EVERGLADES

Although no one had come to see her graduate, nevertheless, while waiting for an offer of a teaching position, she had to return to the only home she had. Would a summer at home with Mama be a repeat of former days? She didn't expect the slaps and beatings—they had ceased while she had been in high school. But her grandmother had continued to use those terrible names when talking about Maybelle or when giving an estimate of Katrina's future. However, Mama had changed in some ways. She talked about things she would leave for Katrina—the choice set of silver, the best linens, sets of expensive china. At last she held her granddaughter in high esteem—or seemed to. Katrina beamed with happiness.

Daily she watched the mail. No long envelope with a conference return address arrived for her, only friendly letters. Mama began to fret. Why were they rejecting "her" child? While Katrina wondered too, she made her hiring a subject of prayer. *Dear Lord Jesus, You know I had no idea of becoming an elementary school teacher. But I obeyed Mama and went to Oakwood. I took the only course possible for me—teacher training. Now, dear Father in heaven, I am ready. Place me wherever You want me.* Two days later a long envelope addressed to Miss Katrina V. Nesbitt arrived from the education department of the Florida Conference, asking her to accept a teaching job in a new school in South Bay, the Everglades, Florida.

With dancing eyes and happy voice, Katrina ran into her grandmother's room, waving the letter. "Mama," she cried, "just listen to this!" Then she read the letter aloud. "Isn't that great? I'll be right here in Florida!"

"Well, why not?" Mama said proudly. "You're a Nesbitt, aren't you?"

"Yes, Mama, but I think the real reason is that I asked God to place me where He wanted me. Evidently those children in South Bay need me or I need them or we need each other."

Mrs. Nesbitt looked directly at her and smiled, but said nothing.

Indeed, South Bay's children did need the kind of teacher Katrina proved to be. The Hudson brothers, owners of a large vegetable farm in South Bay, used a great deal of migrant labor. These Christian men noticed how frequently parents put small hands to work picking beans or other crops when they should have been in the public school some distance away. Seeing potentially bright minds being neglected or dwarfed, they decided to do something about it among their workers. Contacting the education department of the Florida Conference of Seventh-day Adventists, they offered to give a building and whatever else deemed necessary if the conference would supply a teacher. To this the conference gladly agreed and extended the invitation to Katrina to be the first teacher.

True to their word, the Hudson brothers allotted one of their four-room cabins near the end of a row for a school and living quarters for the new teacher. Removing the partition between the two front rooms facing the road produced a fairly large classroom. One of the rear rooms became the teacher's home, the other, that of an elderly, single woman.

Two rows of cabins of varying sizes faced each other across a firmly packed dirt road. Outhouses flanked a nearby canal. When Katrina saw her living quarters, she gasped. Never before had she lived in such primitive conditions. A small room contained a cot, a two-burner oil stove, and a small stand for the water pitcher and basin. Beside it stood a slop jar. The clothes closet consisted of some hooks on one of the wooden walls. No ceiling hid the overhead beams and the bare floorboards had no covering. An odd smell permeated the room and immediately set Katrina to scrubbing the floor. However, when she had finished, the room smelled worse. She wrinkled her nose in disgust. Again and again she washed that floor. The boards gleamed, yet the

TEACHER GOES TO THE EVERGLADES

smell intensified. Reasoning that she needed a stronger cleanser, she walked down to the other end of the row of cabins and the company store. To her delight she found the storekeepers to be old friends, Mrs. Ford, Bailey, her husband, and her youngest son, John Richard Ford. After a pleasant chat and the purchase of a recommended cleanser, Katrina returned to her cabin room and again started to work. The woman who shared the cabin with her, hearing her, came to Katrina's door and asked, "What you workin' so hard fur, honey?"

"Oh, good afternoon, Ma'am, I'm trying to rid this room of its awful smell," she answered as she looked up apologetically at her visitor.

The old woman lifted her hands heavenward and laughed, "You ain't never goin' to git that smell out of here with that water. You's usin' sulfur water. Come, child, I'll show you where to git sweet water." Thus began a friendship between youth and age.

By Monday morning Katrina, with some help, had the schoolroom as sparkling as her many-times scrubbed floor. She had the desks, blackboards, and books all properly arranged when 36 children of all ages, sizes, and grade levels trooped in. Shy grins, questioning smiles, and sober faces greeted their new teacher. As Katrina glanced over her brood she mused, *It's a good thing I had to learn how to teach a one-room school during my training at Oakwood.* She smiled as she remembered how she and other students had fussed when the director made them teach several grades in a one-room school setup for a couple of weeks. *Well,* her thoughts continued, *I know how to organize and get the group going.* She successfully put into practice what she had learned at Oakwood College and added a few God-inspired ideas of her own. So well did the year go that the Hudson brothers prepared for a larger group the following year. By the third year a large four-room cabin housed the school. The teacher then lived in a small but much more commodious cabin nearby.

Like the Hudson brothers, Katrina saw the great need existing among her charges and devoted herself completely to them and their parents. Usually the children in the lower grades could attend with fair regularity except when kept at home to baby-sit still younger sisters and brothers while both parents worked in the fields. To solve that problem, she suggested that, except for infants, the children bring their charges to school and all would baby-sit and have lessons, too.

Children who were or should have been in the middle or upper grades frequently absented themselves from school as the work in the fields called them. Recognizing the futility of insisting upon their attendance under the existing circumstances (the need to augment family earnings during the growing season), she began classes for them at six o'clock in the morning. It gave them two hours of uninterrupted classtime before the regular students came for their lessons at eight-thirty. That six-o'clock group were never late and seldom absent. Some of her students became teachers, nurses, one a doctor, others reputable citizens of various communities.

A number of the things that happened to her while teaching in the Everglades would have frightened away a more experienced teacher. Could you sleep with snakes crawling up and down your window screen? Katrina had to learn to accept the noise. One night as she started to drift off to sleep, she felt something heavy fall across her thighs. A large snake had hidden itself in the rafters over her bed. Perhaps the darkened room encouraged it to explore. At any rate, when it landed on the drowsy teacher, she screamed and jerked herself upright. The snake slithered to the floor. Katrina stood upright on the bed, reached over her head to grasp a rafter, and found herself squeezing another snake whose muscles squirmed under her grasp. She doesn't know how she did it, but somehow she pulled her robe from a hook on the wall, stepped onto the washstand, and made a flying leap to the door. Swinging it open, she began to run, not stopping until she reached a lighted cabin three houses away. Between labored breaths, she told about her unwelcome guests. Armed with sticks and a shotgun, two men entered her cabin and checked the room carefully, including the rafters and all corners and possible hiding places to make certain other reptiles did not share the teacher's cabin. A light revealed a big snake crawling off into some bushes. One shot and its life ended. Evidently the creatures had followed Katrina out through the door. Certain that there would

TEACHER GOES TO THE EVERGLADES

be no further snake invasions, the men led Katrina back to her quarters where she slept fitfully the rest of the night.

On another occasion a rat got in while Katrina slept and sampled four fingers of her left hand. Either the taste didn't suit the rat or Katrina woke up before the culprit could settle down to feasting. The rat had caused no pain; it had only disturbed her enough to arouse her. It is claimed that rats anesthetize their victims and that often the wound will not heal. Katrina's finger tips were only red and uncomfortable. The next day the children heard about the rat attack upon their teacher. They told their parents, and in no time the adults rat-proofed her cabin.

The snakes were everywhere. They hung over the privy doors, stretched ropelike in the shrubbery, hid among the bushes, under stones and rocks, in cabins—everywhere. This teacher who had screamed and thrown away her blackberries at the sight of a harmless black snake that slithered out of her way soon lost her fear of the reptiles. "God took away my fear and protected me all the time I worked in the Everglades," she explains today. "Now, however, I can't bear the sight of the creatures, not even in pictures or on TV. They give me the creeps."

Truly God must have removed her fear, for at the last cabin in which she lived, a king snake daily stretched itself across the second step leading into her cabin. People say that it will kill all other kinds of snakes, hence its name, "king." To enter or leave Katrina's cabin, one simply skipped over her guardian snake. It never harmed anyone. Could God have sent it to protect her?

Others were not always so fortunate. While waiting for their parents to come in from the fields, children living near the school often played on or near the school grounds after lessons ceased. One afternoon Katrina sat alone in the classroom correcting papers and making plans for the next day's work. Suddenly the play noises stopped. Little Manona came tumbling into the room crying, "Kitty bite, pretty kitty bite Julia Mae!"

Katrina rushed out, followed by the child, Manona, whose sister, Julia Mae, tearfully showed the teacher the bite on her forearm. The shape of the bite loudly proclaimed "snakebite."

"Julia Mae, show me where you saw the kitty," the teacher asked the still-sobbing child.

KATRINA STANDS ALONE

She pointed to a pile of rocks among some tall grasses. With a long stick Katrina poked among the rocks until a small yellow-, red- and black-ringed snake glided toward another hiding place. Commanding the children to step back, she succeeded in striking the reptile and killing it with one blow before it could escape again. Then holding it up on the stick so that all the children could plainly see it, their teacher warned, "Never, never go near Julia Mae's kitty. It is not a cat. It's a very dangerous, poisonous snake."

Deeply worried, Katrina placed the bitten child on one of the school steps so that her wounded arm could hang down. She sent one of the students standing nearby for soap and water and washed the wound. Manona ran to get their father who had just driven in from the field. He came immediately and carried Julia Mae to his truck. Manona climbed in with them. The children's father asked Katrina to please drive the truck while he tried to give his little girl artificial respiration, for she had lost consciousness.

Katrina had never driven a car, much less a truck, but she had watched her uncles drive both. With furrowed brow and rapidly beating heart, she took the wheel, sending up a silent prayer for help and reciting to herself one of her favorite Bible verses: "I can do all things through Christ which strengtheneth me" (Phil. 4:13). Turning on the ignition, she pressed down on the accelerator, and they lurched off to the hospital 40 miles away. A white handkerchief tied to the truck alerted a state trooper of the emergency, and he led them, siren wailing, all the way to their destination. Katrina nearly knocked the building down before she managed to stop the truck. The hospital staff rushed Julia Mae into emergency, where the doctors worked hard to save her life. Knowing the kind of snake that had bitten her made their task easier. The girl recovered, grew up, and later became a nurse. However, she has a nervous reaction at the sight of snakes.

On another occasion when dismissing her pupils, Katrina warned, "Go straight home! Don't get near the canals."

"Yes, Miss Nesbitt," they chorused. But on such a lovely afternoon what harm could it do to sit by the canal, talk, and play a bit before going home? So five little girls sat on the bank of a canal, talking, laughing, and playing until one of them slid halfway down the slippery bank. Little hands reached to pull her back, but all they could do was hold her hands. They lacked the strength to lift her.

At the school, their teacher, busy putting things in order, had a persistent feeling that she should take a walk by that particular canal. She tried ignoring the impression, but relentlessly it continued to come. Finally she decided, just for piece of mind, to stroll in that direction. Besides, a walk would be good on such a beautiful day. When the children saw her coming, they loosened their grasps on their classmate's hands and she plunged, feet first, into the canal.

Seeing the children just standing there wide-eyed, speechless, and open-mouthed, Katrina knew instinctively something had to be wrong. Hastening up to the group, she glimpsed one of her pupils vainly trying to get out of the water. But a white-mouthed water moccasin swam ever closer and closer, preventing her from getting ashore. Without a thought her teacher pulled off her shoes and slid down the bank into the murky water. She grabbed the child and threw her up the bank, telling her companions to catch her. Then she had to confront the circling snake. "I must not panic," she told herself. A short distance away a couple of logs spanned the canal as a kind of bridge. Katrina swam to them, took a giant leap upward, grabbed one of the logs, and pulled herself to safety. Although she had ruined her new yellow dress, she had saved the little girl. No need for scolding or punishment. All five little girls had learned a valuable lesson in the need for obedience.

In spite of the generous provisions of the Hudson brothers for the schooling of the children of their workers, a few did not attend nor did they go to the public schools. Children under 16 could not work in the fields legally. Anyone hiring them would be fined. Such unlawfully working children received no wages personally. What they earned became a part of the family's income. It took the rumor that the truant officer would be around to get such youngsters into a classroom. On such occasions, 80 or more children would crowd Katrina's school for two or three days. They included those coming in from nearby farms and who should have been in the public schools.

After three years of loving and teaching the appreciative Everglades children, she felt the need for a change. Having worked hard, she had learned much, and felt the power of God's leading in her life and work. She had inspired children, youth, and many of their parents to raise their sights and expectations, to strive for excellence. Besides valiantly upholding the Nesbitt name, she had raised her own self-image, and proved that as a Christian worker she too could aspire to excellence.

9

CITY BOUND

Knowing of her success in starting the South Bay School in the Everglades, the educational secretary of the Florida Conference asked her to reopen a school in New Smyrna Beach. It sounded challenging. The school would be in a small city environment, a welcome change after three years of isolation on a large plantation-like farm. And if Mama needed her at any time, it would be easy to get home. Katrina accepted the position.

Home for the summer, she told her grandmother about the change. "I'll be able to come home quickly if you need me. Trains and buses run between New Smyrna Beach and here often."

"Why didn't you ask to teach in our school here?" Mama retorted.

"Oh, Mama, I need more experience to teach in a large school like ours."

"I don't see why. Teaching is teaching."

"Yes, Mama, I know, but, well, I'd rather wait until I've had much more experience before tackling the large schools."

"Scared, eh?"

"Not really, Mama, but if I taught here now, it would be as 'Miss Lois's daughter,' not me. I want to make it on my own and then when I've made a name for myself as a teacher, perhaps come back and teach here, maybe even be principal of our Miami school."

Mama grunted, looked pleased, but said nothing.

Shortly before time for school to open, Katrina left Miami for New Smyrna Beach. She would room with the Bookhart family, a plan her grandmother warmly approved of. Mrs. Bookhart met Katrina's train, and in a little while the young teacher had settled in her stately, two-storied home.

KATRINA STANDS ALONE

After a pleasant night's sleep, Katrina eagerly looked forward to viewing her new school. How big would it be? How many windows for light and air? What kind of bulletin board space would be available? What kind of playground would the children have? Plenty of questions urgently needed answers in order for her to plan. Mrs. Bookhart led her to a small, attractive frame church a short distance away. They entered the silent vestibule and walked up a few steps. Then Mrs. Bookhart swung open the large doors, revealing the orderly rows of pews and the pulpit with its usual furniture. Doors to the right and left of the platform led to the vestry and to the choir room. Katrina expressed admiration for the simple, attractive, well-kept edifice, then asked, "Where are the schoolrooms?"

"Schoolroom?" Mrs. Bookhart said in a questioning tone, then added, "you're looking at it."

Katrina slumped into the nearest pew, her mouth open. "You mean hold regular school classes in the nave of the church?"

"Yes, Katrina, we're tired of waiting to build or buy a separate building. Year after year our children go to schools in which our God can't even be mentioned. We have to begin somewhere or lose all our children."

Katrina's eyes assumed a faraway expression as she tried to digest the news. After a brief pause she said, "Thank you for telling me. Would you please leave me here alone for a while? I'll find my way back to the house."

Sensing the young woman's feelings, Mrs. Bookhart replied, "Certainly, stay as long as you wish." She added, "This is only a temporary thing. Our church will continue to work for a separate building just as soon as possible. We felt we had to begin again somehow. I'm sure the members will be happy to do anything they can for you. Just be sure the outside door is locked when you leave."

After her landlady left, Katrina sat quietly musing to herself. *If we have school in the main part of the church, won't that mar the children's sense of reverence for God's house? Where are the children to sit to write their lessons? How can I motivate them to learn without equipment, room decorations, and bulletin boards? Where can I or they set up little projects?* Facing so many

CITY BOUND

hindrances, she dropped to her knees and cried out, "Lord, help me! I cannot succeed in this endeavor alone. This is Your work. These are Your people, trying to save their children for You. Please give me wisdom for this task. In Your Son Jesus' name." As she continued to kneel, a feeling of peace overshadowed her. She knew that God had heard and answered her prayer. New Smyrna Beach would have a good school year.

She worked hard, prayed much, and encouraged herself frequently by repeating Philippians 4:13. True, the children had to sit or kneel on the floor and use the pews as writing desks when table space gave out. But with ingenuity, she managed to assemble decorations and bulletin board materials without desecrating walls or furniture. The novelty of the situation intrigued those children who had previously attended public school, and the beginners knew nothing else. All learned, none failed, God blessed. Nor did Katrina keep so busy that she found no time to exercise her selflessness. When she heard of a family of children often abandoned for days by their parents, she took the 6-year-old girl in, kept her, took her to school, and paid her school expenses. Other members of the church gave care to the other children in that family.

Life for the teacher held other things besides work. A small group of teenagers belonging to the church took pleasure in bicycle riding. Katrina often joined them, sometimes riding as far as Daytona Beach 15 miles away. There they met the Daytona church teen group and often picnicked with them.

The school year drew to a close. Pleased with the results from their little school, the church redoubled its efforts to secure a building as more parents planned to send their children the following year. But Miss Nesbitt would not be there. She had accepted a position in a three-teacher school in Jacksonville, a real step up the professional ladder. Then an added bonus— Zelma Hodge, Katrina's beloved "Lama"—had returned to Jacksonville after the death of her husband, and now lived in the old homestead with her sister and family. In the move she would exchange the hospitality of the Bookharts for a renewal of life among longtime friends, the Palmers and Mrs. Hodge. How could she refuse?

KATRINA STANDS ALONE

Accordingly, the 1944 school year found her teaching grades one through four in Jacksonville. An Oakwood schoolmate, Mabel Rollins, held forth in grades five and six, and Charles Cunningham, son of the beloved "Mother dear" of Oakwood, took care of grades seven and eight as a teacher-principal. The association with other teachers helped her sharpen her teaching skills as the three shared ideas. Lama, a teacher of many years' experience, also gave her helpful suggestions.

A good rapport existed between the community and the Jacksonville school, and a few nonmembers (of the church) enrolled their children there. A next-door neighbor decided to send her youngest to Katrina's room. David enjoyed his experiences in the private school and learned rapidly and well. His mother—pleased with his progress in reading and math plus all his Bible and moral teaching—allowed him to continue in that school until he graduated. He then went to Oakwood Academy and College, graduated from the Theology Department, and became a successful pastor. David was among the first of many ministers and pastors whose educational journey began in Katrina Nesbitt's room.

She did not forget home, keeping in touch with Mama by letter and by occasional weekend visits. However, she never wanted to stay again under that roof of fear and abuse. Mama always seemed self-sufficient, and Katrina vowed she would be too. But unknown to her, Mrs. Nesbitt had been ailing for some time. Finally she decided to go to Riverside Sanitarium and Hospital in Nashville, Tennessee, for a checkup. Upon examining her, the doctor discovered a fibroid tumor and recommended immediate surgery.

As soon as she knew she had to have the operation, Mama Lois sent for her granddaughter to come and stay with her at the hospital. When Katrina received the message, her first impulse was to hurry to her. Then she began to think. *If I go now it will upset the entire school program. I'll need to stay until she is able to travel and go home. Then she'll probably need special care at home for a while. What should I do? It's almost impossible to get a substitute teacher, and Mabel can't possibly teach my four grades with 25 children and her large number in grades five and*

CITY BOUND

six, too. Maybe Charles could teach a few of her classes along with his own work. Even so, it would still be too much for Mabel. Um, if we got a sub, would she know how to work with my special children—the shy little girl from that poor family; Tom, the aggressive one who knows no better way to get attention; and my little Miss who thinks that being beautiful and cute does away with the need to work and learn?

Katrina shared her dilemma with Lama. "I guess I'm a bit rusty," the older woman said thoughtfully, "but I suppose I could sub for you."

"Oh! will you?"

Giving Katrina a little hug, she replied, "No, I've a better idea. I'll go to Lois. We're old friends, and I'm sure I can be more help to her in the hospital than you can. I'll explain to her that you wanted to come. I think I can manage her better than I can a bunch of noisy children."

However, before Lama could get to Riverside, Mrs. Nesbitt had been rushed into surgery, operated on successfully, and after a stay in intensive care, wheeled back into her private room. A few days later while Lama went to dinner, leaving the patient alone briefly, Mrs. Nesbitt rang for a nurse. Since one did not come immediately, she tried to get out of bed on her own, only to have a stroke and fall. When the nurse finally arrived and found her on the floor, she summoned the doctor and head nurse. They did everything possible for the patient, and she gradually recovered.

Lama stayed with Lois at Riverside until the doctor released her and then traveled with her to Miami. There she helped her to adjust to home surroundings, saw to it that she secured the special shoe the doctor recommended for her shortened leg, and arranged for household and nursing help for her friend. By the end of the school year Mama could walk quite well except for a slight limp. One by one every vestige of the stroke left except a slight limp and the darkening of skin. Her general health improved greatly, and she felt like her old self. However, when the Jacksonville school closed for the summer and Katrina came home for a vacation, Mama leaned heavily on her in spite of all the help at her disposal. It became evident to Katrina that even if her grandmother were in perfect health, she would never really fully release her. She had failed to show a mother's love, yet expected a daughter's selfless devotion.

Teaching in a larger school setting had convinced Katrina that she needed further study. She read about new things happening in education, of new methods of teaching based upon psychological research. Wanting to give God her best service, she believed more training would enhance her skills. She hoped Mama would understand why she must get back to college. The easiest way would be to return to Oakwood, which had become a four-year accredited degree-granting institution where she could obtain a bachelor's degree in education. At the end of her second year at the Jacksonville school, she bade her students, coworkers, and the friendly Palmers, including Lama, goodbye and returned to her home in Miami.

10

BACK TO COLLEGE

One evening during a long pause in the conversation between her grandmother and her brother Marshall, visiting from nearby Deerfield, Katrina said, "Mama, everything has been done for your comfort and you are well now. I would like to go back to college and get a degree in education, then I'll be prepared to teach anywhere in the United States."

"Humph!" the woman grunted. "You got too big for Florida?"

"No, Mama. I'd hoped you'd understand. Since I've been teaching, I realize more fully how important the profession is. How much our church schools need good teachers. I want to be the very best one I can be. Mama, don't you see, the more I know, the more I can help our boys and girls?"

Uncle Marshall interrupted them. "You don't need any more education. You need to stay here and take care of your grandmother."

Katrina's temper flared as she thought, *What right has he to interfere?* Quickly controlling herself, she answered briskly, "Mama has three living sons. She has done everything for them, given them anything they wanted—money, cars, land, offers of college education. Yet only one of them went to college, and he didn't finish. Surely three of them can look after their own mother."

"Lois raised you, fed and clothed you, sent you to school," Marshall retorted. "Now you need to stay home and take care of her."

"Uncle Marshall, I don't want to be disrespectful, but you don't understand. Papa loved and provided for me. Mama did what she did because of him and her pride in appearances. She never loved me nor my mother. However, I have no intentions of forsaking her. I'll be available to her whenever she truly needs me. If I'm not available, I'll see that she is taken care of, just as I did when she had to go to Riverside, and Lama went in my place. Papa left Mama well provided for, but with more education, if ever necessary, I could better care for Mama financially."

"Humph!" her great-uncle responded. "You're just trying to weasel out of staying home."

Mama sat mute, expressionless. "Uncle Marshall and Mama," the granddaughter continued, "I've been teaching several years now, time enough to test myself and discover how much more I need to learn in order to do a more effective job. I want to go as far as I can so that I can give God the best service."

"How do you expect to get all this schooling?" Mrs. Nesbitt demanded. "I'll not pay your way."

"I'll work my way through, as I did my second year at Oakwood. Lots of people do. It will be hard, but with God's help, and I hope your prayers, I'll succeed." So saying, she left the room with a prayer in her heart, "Father, help them to understand."

During the summer Katrina worked as a maid in a Miami Beach hotel. With her earnings and with what she had put aside from her teaching she had enough to start at Oakwood as a junior college student. She registered for work in the culinary department, to the delight of the matron and to the older students who had heard about her cooking. For a couple of months Mama gave some financial assistance, then abruptly it ceased without any explanation. However, by putting in long work hours and cutting down on the number of courses taken each semester, in three years Katrina managed to complete the two years of classes required for a degree.

In spite of her heavy work load, she found time for fun and friendships. Her dormitory mates affectionately called her "Bopps" and looked to her as both friend and leader. When Oakwood's Department of Education organized the first Future Teachers of America (FTA) Club in the state of Alabama, Katrina became a charter member. The FTA, an affiliate of the National Education Association (NEA) — at the time a strictly nonpolitical, educational body — gave prestige to students training to be teachers. Oakwood's FTA did much to enhance the campus as well as to bring in outstanding lecturers and entertainers. The FTA members raised funds for the guests through various activities in which Katrina always took part.

In the forties and early fifties the college provided little organized gymnastics or sports for women. However, the Education Department had a required course for its teacher-trainees entitled "Exercises and Games for Children." It included lessons in tumbling (women only). The activities shocked some of the old, reserved campus residents and intrigued the male students who could not take the class. A gastric ulcer barred Katrina from the tumbling lessons. However, she enjoyed watching her dormmates practice in the long halls of their building. She could at least laugh at their spills and applaud their successes. In this way she shared their fun.

During those last student years several faculty members tried to establish a mother-daughter relationship with Katrina. She politely held them all at bay, sensing their interest in her grew out of her grandmother's wealth. However, Katrina still longed for someone she could love as a mother and who would love her in return. She knew that her friends Mildred, Katie, and even Julie had accepted their junior college women's dean and called her "mother" or "mommie" back during the 1939-1940 school year. Although they had included her in their after-lights-out sessions with the dean, she had not been able to let herself use that special word. Now that same person chaired the Education Department and taught many of the education and psychology classes, giving the students plenty of opportunity to observe her. Katrina noted that although she demanded thoroughness, she never yelled at a student or called anyone stupid, that she carefully answered questions and patiently pointed out mistakes, reexplained when necessary, and assured the student he or she could do well. She never became so busy that she could not see a student after class, in her office, or even in her apartment. All knew she cared. Katrina felt ready to trust her. After a brief, desultory conversation one afternoon in the dean's apartment, Katrina softly asked, "Will you be my mother?"

"If you wish it, I'd be happy to be mother to a fine young

KATRINA STANDS ALONE

woman like you." No hugs or handshakes, but a steady eye between two shy people. At last Katrina had found a surrogate mother. With such certainty did she believe in the relationship that she had it legalized with the stipulation that, as an heir to her grandparents, Andrew and Lois Nesbitt, she would retain the surname Nesbitt.

Katrina did not become "teacher's pet," however. When she showed her new mother a grade card with a D in one of her subjects, her new mother said, "For shame! Don't you cross my doorsill again until you bring me a better grade in that subject!" Katrina stormed angrily out of the room, raced down the stairs, and with a bang slammed the screen door. At the next marking period, however, she returned, waving her report card bearing an A in every subject.

"Great! That's more like it. I knew you could do it. That is why I challenged you. My daughters must always do their best, even when they don't feel like it. How can you teach others to strive for perfection if you do not do so yourself? Always remember, you are preparing to work for the Master Teacher, Jesus Christ. Only your best is good enough."

The years of work and study ended gloriously for Katrina, an honor student. Mama Nesbitt did not come to see her receive her degree, but Uncle Joseph and a cousin witnessed her moment of triumph.

11

SHE SAID, "NO!" GOD SAID, "YES!"

Graduation over, she, her cousin, and her uncle Joseph returned to Miami. The car stopped in front of the old familiar home. Katrina walked up the porch steps and through the door where Mama stood waiting, a smile lighting up her gray eyes.

The tired young teacher spent a pleasant summer at home with Mama who said little but seemed to be proud of her grandchild's accomplishments. A Nesbitt, one of her own, had brought honor to the Nesbitt name. She had become an educated person of impeccable character, her name well known and respected at Oakwood College, the Florida Conference, and in her home community. No longer could Mama hurl prophecies of worthlessness against the degree-holding Miss Katrina Viola Nesbitt. Still habit stayed strong: no hugs, kisses, or words of endearment passed between them. But attitudes seemed to have changed. Katrina could look and act happy, something she had not dared to do before for fear Mama would say something insulting or set her to an unpleasant task. Now Mama showed her linens, silverware, and expensive china that would be a part of her inheritance. She assured her that she would share equally with her uncles the house and all other properties just as Papa had planned.

Summer ended, and time came to go back to work. During her last half year as a senior at college, education secretaries from several conferences had interviewed the seniors for possible placement in their respective conferences. The secretary of the Florida Conference already knew Katrina's capabilities as a teacher. He offered her the principal-teacher role in the two-teacher, nine-grade St. Petersburg School. She accepted it despite the fact that several other conferences were interested in her.

Katrina learned that her associate teacher would be a former schoolmate, Pearlester Curry. They had been good Oakwood friends, and Katrina looked forward to a happy experience in St. Petersburg. Pearlester and Katrina worked well together as a team. However, Katrina discovered that, as in other places she had taught, some parents, though eager to provide a Christian education for their children, were not always able to do so financially. The Curry-Nesbitt team often aided such children by raising funds through the church and by personally helping to secure suitable clothing and occasionally food. The have-nots continued to be Katrina's special concern.

Her influence went beyond the classroom. She roomed with the Mitchell family, who had three children. As a result of the quality of her work in school and her Christian lifestyle in their home, Mr. Mitchell accepted Christ, gave up worldly habits, and did everything possible to make his family happy. Even the way he conducted his grocery business changed. The community noticed, and business grew.

Katrina spent two good years teaching with Pearlester in the St. Petersburg School. The parents were cooperative and the children highly motivated to learn well. The conference education secretary rated the school as one of the best in the state. But Katrina grew restless. An unhappy incident had so upset her that she decided she could no longer remain in that setting. In spite of her success and the pleas of parents and children, she decided to leave. She would go to work somewhere, save her money, then study to be that dietitian she'd wanted to be in the first place. Reaching her decision, she threw up her arms, tossed back her head, and exclaimed, "No more teaching school until I teach what I want—dietetics in a high school or college."

She planned that upon leaving St. Petersburg, she would visit her friend Mildred Evelyn-Jones, then living in Wilmington, Delaware. But before she could close her school, she received an invitation from Katie Walker, who, after a long delay in getting back to college, would graduate that May with a B.S. in secretarial science and accounting. En route to Delaware, Katrina

SHE SAID, "NO!" GOD SAID, "YES!"

stopped in Huntsville, Alabama, for Katie's graduation. After it she planned to spend the rest of the summer with Mildred, perhaps find a job in Wilmington, and stay there indefinitely.

As she walked across the campus shortly after her arrival, she met the college president, F. L. Peterson. After cordial greetings and inquiries about her grandmother, he said, "I've just finished dictating a letter, inviting you to teach here next school year, but you are here before the letter can get into the mail. We would like to have you in our laboratory school as a supervising teacher of the lower grades. Will you come?"

Katrina stared at him in amazement, not knowing what to say. She had already made up her mind—no more teaching elementary school grades. Her stop at Oakwood was only a break on her way to something—anything—different that hopefully would lead to high school or college teaching. However, to be offered the chance to teach at her alma mater—what an honor! What should she say?

Seeing how stunned she was by his offer, the president suggested, "Well, Miss Katrina, you give the idea some thought and let me know in a few days. The director of the department recommended you highly. She believes you are right for the position and so do I." So saying, he walked away.

"Thank you, President Peterson," Katrina managed to reply, her thoughts still in a whirl. *Mother recommended me for this opening and didn't ask or tell me about it? She has trained a number of good teachers. Why did she not choose one of them with more experience? But, if she thinks I'm good enough, how can I say "No"? Can I really make a good supervising teacher?* As soon as possible she sought counsel from the director of the Education Department and finally decided to accept the invitation. Never teach elementary school again? The Master Teacher had a different idea. She would see several more years of such service.

12

SUPERVISING TEACHER

As she had planned, Katrina went on to visit Mildred. A week after her arrival in Delaware, she received a telegram. *What now?* she wondered. Opening it she read, "I need you, come home, I'm sick." Signed: Lois Nesbitt.

Immediately Katrina made arrangements for the long ride to Miami. As the train rattled along, she wondered, *Has Mama had another stroke? Has she fallen and perhaps broken her hip? Maybe she's had a serious heart attack. Is she in the hospital or confined at home?* When Katrina arrived home, she found her grandmother her usual self—no worse than when she had seen her a few short weeks before.

"I felt lonely and wanted you to come home," Mama explained. "I thought you had deserted me."

"No, Mama, I will never desert you," her granddaughter assured her, "but, as I told you before I left, I went to visit Mildred and possibly find work that would pay enough so I can save money to get the training for what I've always wanted to be, a dietitian."

"Sly way of getting out of working in the church, I see."

"Not necessarily, Mama. You know the church has a wonderful health message. If I'm prepared, I might be able to teach principles of healthful dieting at one of our schools or sanitariums."

"Sounds possible."

Katrina continued good-naturedly, "I've got good news for you, Mama."

"Good news? Whatever is it?"

"President Peterson has asked me to teach in the college laboratory school and supervise student teachers working in grades one through four. I've accepted. That's why you did not receive a big letter from me, just a card. I had to give that offer much thought."

"Well, that is news! Where will you stay? In the dormitory?"

"No, Mama, it's all settled. I'm to share an apartment with the chairperson of the department, Miss Burrell."

"Oh! I've known her for a long time. She will keep you straight."

Mama, at last satisfied, willingly relinquished to another the responsibility for the moral turpitude of her grandchild. However, the physical and emotional scars from her treatment of her granddaughter remained.

Katrina arrived at the college about 10 days before school began. It gave her time to settle in the apartment, to be briefed about her duties, and to set her classroom in readiness for registration day. About the same time the rest of the staff returned from vacation and together they, with the director-principal, agreed upon plans for the school year. On opening day classrooms and teachers were ready. Children arrived scrubbed, combed and brushed, and carefully dressed. Mothers brought their beginners—some shy and timid, others eager to join their older siblings in the adventure called school. Katrina has a knack for putting children at ease. Soon smiles and laughter replaced fear and tears.

School soon settled into a comfortable routine. The children were happy and learning well under their new teacher. Soon it would be November, time to begin planning and rehearsing for a Thanksgiving program. Then came the unexpected—another telegram from home.

> MAMA DIED THIS MORNING
> FARE AT TELEGRAPH OFFICE
> Signed: Joseph Nesbitt
> Date: Oct. 30, 1950

Katrina left for Miami that afternoon. Joseph, the only son still living in Miami, had called his brothers and made the immediate funeral arrangements.

After Mama's interment Katrina looked for the special things she had promised her. However, all she found were a few pieces of a willowware set and the everyday silver. All else had disappeared, even things Katrina had left for her grandmother to keep for her, such as school trophies and awards. She returned to Oakwood deeply grieved that now with Mama's death she would never be able to get her to accept Maybelle and with that acceptance come to really love Maybelle's child. Also she regretted that everything she had held dear had been taken from her. Sometime later, her uncles sold the homestead and other properties without consulting her, a legal heir. They never shared the proceeds from the sales with her. Convinced she had no real family to turn to, she clung all the more closely to her adoptive mother. Her college friends became as real sisters to her. Deeply hurt, she focused her thoughts upon the remembered kindnesses of the Cravattes—given mostly surreptitiously—during her childhood. She knew her mother's people had sympathized with and loved her. Although Mama had kept her from having any close association with her half-sisters, she knew them and longed to be with them. Someday she would. It became her long-term goal.

Instead of complaining about her situation, she threw herself completely again into her teaching. For 13 years she taught grades 1-4 at the Oakwood College Laboratory School. She brought to the task all her skills and expertise. She added to them by attending summer school at Danbury, Connecticut, and in New York at Columbia University's Teachers College. Constantly she worked hand in hand with the director-principal, who kept abreast of things in the educational world by wide reading and much graduate study. Katrina and her "mother" not only shared an apartment, they also shared information. Assisted by other teachers in the school, Katrina carried on the teacher-training classes during the director's absence.

In spite of the harmony existing among the teachers and the director-principal of the laboratory school, several problems persisted. A major one involved operating expenses. The entire college was in the process of growth and each department clamored for funds for upgrading, making it difficult for the administration to set department priorities. Teachers, especially in the laboratory school, often had to improvise. This, however, did not prove to be all bad. In some cases it helped by demonstrating to students how to cope when in similar circumstances in the small schools where some of them might later be teaching. Katrina, a master at inventing with substitute materials, frequently demonstrated this skill to her students. Strange that she, brought up in a home of luxury, should know how to put materials often consigned to the waste bins to practical and productive use.

Another problem centered around socioeconomic differences among her pupils. In addition to teaching all the subjects for the four grades, she had to make learning possible for children on three different levels: (1) those with a wide range of previous learning experiences, (2) those with fewer experiences but who learned easily, and (3) children from the surrounding countryside with, in many cases, only a meager exposure to books, travel, or cultural experiences. The latter were not stupid. Quite the contrary, they were country-wise, many with keen minds. It took skill to integrate such groups into a whole, but Katrina succeeded beautifully.

Poverty caused more problems. Many married couples brought their children with them to college, hoping to get enough work to support their own education and that of their children. Numerous sacrifices managed to keep Dad in college and the children in the laboratory school, but some of the children often faced days of inadequate food and clothing. In such cases they became Katrina's immediate concern. She believes that self-image is vital to learning. How can a hungry or poorly dressed child have a worthwhile image of himself? Her pleas to the matron often procured milk and other nourishing foods for such needy children.

When Katrina observed a child in her room coming to school ragged, inadequately clothed, or poorly shod, she talked to the parents. If they were unable to provide the needed clothing, she would buy or make the needed garment and purchase shoes, sneakers, socks, and underwear. In some instances she bought coats and sweaters. Whenever her students were to appear on programs, she saw to it that the poor child would be as carefully dressed as any other. She would sit at her machine and turn out four or five dresses from material she had purchased. None of the children were ever embarrassed before the public. The lessons in dressmaking she had had to take as a part of her home economics studies in high school now came in handy.

Even during the long summer vacations the children remained on her mind. While vacationing with friends, she collected clothes, many of them new, from friends whose children either had too much or had outgrown the garments. She kept the garments on hand and altered them as needed. No doubt her interest in the underprivileged child had been inborn and continued from her own childhood when she gave away her expensive clothes and shoes that her grandparents provided for her. Her caring went beyond her own students. When the husband of her college friend, Mildred Evelyn-Jones, left her with two children, the youngest a girl of 6, Katrina came to the rescue. While performing her regular duties and filling in for the director, away on leave of absence, Katrina brought little Carla to stay with her at Oakwood. As "Aunt 'Trina," she kept the child, sent her to school, and furnished all her needs. It gave Mildred time to secure work as a public school teacher and also make plans for her son.

As the supervising teacher, she gave constructive criticism that lent itself to successful teaching. No matter how well a student prepares, he or she is always anxious when approaching the initial teaching experience. The student-teacher is responsible for the order, discipline, and the learning of the children. The judges are both the students and the supervising teacher. Katrina's manner, as well as her method, helped greatly to put the student-teacher at ease. Privately she discussed their errors and made suggestions to correct them. Often she would lead the student-teacher to discover ways to handle a tense situation himself or herself. In correcting mistakes in teaching, Katrina tried diligently never to embarrass the student-teacher, nor would she let the mistake harm her children. Often she used the mistakes as learning devices both for the teacher and the class. She gave extra time to her student-teachers who had instructional or discipline problems. When she discovered a problem of general interest, she brought it to the attention of the director who could then discuss it further in a college methods or management class.

SUPERVISING TEACHER

As the department grew, demands came for training in secondary education. After careful study and in consultation with the dean of the college, the chairperson of the Education Department made up a program for that area of teaching and opened up two special classes for interested students. All went well for a while, then a person working in the department began to push hard for the secondary education program, and elementary education majors came under pressure to switch to the secondary-level program. Some of them became so confused that they came to Katrina, at the time substituting for the director who was absent on leave, for advice. In her inimitable quiet way she helped the bewildered students realize the importance of their choice, and they continued happily with their preparations as elementary school teachers.

13

MORE STATELY DWELLINGS

The laboratory school building that housed the elementary school and the principal's office had been built many years earlier. The two-story frame structure had outgrown its usefulness during the influx of students pouring in after World War II and the following baby boom. Methods of teaching had changed and recent studies in psychology had greatly influenced educational approach. Ideas on discipline and classroom management had made necessary a widely different environment for teaching and learning. Trying to fit such new pedagogy into the framework of that old building compared with the Bible illustration of putting new wine in old bottles or mending an old garment with new cloth (Mark 2:21, 22). To educate children well—or to try to—and at the same time prepare knowledgeable teachers capable of coping in any system of education requires opportunities to study, observe, and practice in facilities with adequate equipment in properly constructed buildings. They are as essential as a well-planned curriculum or course of study.

For years the laboratory school teachers, including Katrina, joined their director in presenting the needs of their department—especially a new, modern building—to the college business manager and the president. The latter sympathized with their requests for a more adequate building, but other things took precedence—new dormitories, housing for married students, updating of farm and dairy, improving bakery and campus store, and making more parking space. President Peterson's administration took care of many of the needs. When he left, the drive for a new laboratory school continued under the new president, Garland Millet. Finally the prayers, pleas, and tears of all concerned at last produced results. Under President Millet the new building took shape. A sprawling one-story brick building

MORE STATELY DWELLINGS

arose on a slight knoll in a much better location. It sat back from the main road, eliminating a traffic hazard and also providing a larger playground area.

The second story of the old frame building had been used variously for college classes, had been left vacant temporarily, had housed a retired professor who came with his wife to teach a year or two, and then had been converted into two apartments for single teachers. Here Katrina and her adoptive mother made their home and entertained students and out-of-town guests. However, instead of each living in half the area, they converted the entire floor into one apartment and shared it equally. Curtains, potted plants, and decorative floor coverings made the place look cozy. However, nothing could stop the ravages of time as they made their stealthy and continuous raids upon the building. In spite of all that the maintenance personnel and carpenter could do, they urgently needed better living quarters.

The college built new houses for faculty, but not for Katrina and her mother. Requests followed requests. Even students asked "Why?" At last a new house became ready for them. The college administration told them to pack up and be ready to move on a certain day. The day arrived but the school changed its plans. Again the management set another day, and again it had to be postponed. For the third and fourth time the same thing happened. Meanwhile Katrina and her mother waited, all packed up in boxes, trunks, and suitcases for weeks.

Early one evening Katrina came in and found her adoptive mother standing in a closet, silently weeping with frustration. For the umpteenth time she had had to unpack and repack materials she needed for a class. Angrily Katrina rushed out of the building in search of help. She found a ready ally in Dr. E. E. Rogers, husband of Katrina's college friend Mildred Strawgn. When Katrina told him of her mother's frustration, he remarked, "We can't have Mom in tears! Come, let's talk to the business manager immediately." Whatever they said got action. Within a week Katrina and her mother became the occupants of a new five-room house.

Two years later the director of the Education Department accepted a call to the denominational headquarters in Washing-

KATRINA STANDS ALONE

ton, D.C., as coeditor of a series of readers for the parochial schools. Her duties fell upon Katrina's shoulders until the college could find a replacement. Since she had taught in the Southern Union nearly 20 years, Katrina, well-known to the leaders, received invitations to attend union meetings as representative of Oakwood College. The Education Department of Southern College, at Collegedale, Tennessee, also invited her to their general meetings. In spite of her successes, after 20 years of service, she decided for personal reasons to resign and seek work in some other section of the U.S.

14

NORTHWARD BOUND

No need to return to Miami. Both Papa and Mama Nesbitt no longer lived. The homestead had been sold, her uncles married and in different states. Only Joseph and his wife, Mary, and their family still lived in Miami. Although a joint heir with her uncles, Katrina had nothing—not even the lots she had been purchasing in nearby Daytona Beach through her cousin McAfee. She had sent regular amounts from her teaching salary to Mama with the request that she forward it to her cousin McAfee. For some reason the cousin never received the money. Katrina lost the property. Except for Joe and Mary, she had no caring relative on her father's side, no home in Miami, and no nest egg. Resolutely she turned her back upon the city of her birth and set off for Washington, D.C., and Delaware to be with friends and to seek work. Soon after arriving in D.C., she received a telephone call from Emerton Whigby, education secretary of the Northeastern Conference, inviting her to be a principal-teacher at a school in Rochester, New York. She asked for time to think it over. *Do I really want to teach in another parochial school?* she asked herself.

After a short visit with Mildred in Delaware, she returned to D.C. Camp meeting time had arrived and her mother had an invitation to speak at the Northeastern Conference camp meeting. Katrina decided to drive her mother up to Hyde Park, New York, where the session would be held. While there she met a number of her former Oakwood schoolmates, among them Emerton Whigby. He pressed for an answer to his telephone call, asking her to take the Rochester position. Unable to resist, she accepted. After mother and daughter returned to Washington, Katrina took a trip to Rochester to see the school and to find living quarters for herself. Then she went back to D.C., where she caught a train for

KATRINA STANDS ALONE

Huntsville, Alabama, to pack her furniture.

Finished with that, she took a train north, this time for the school in Rochester. Immediately she went to the apartment already arranged for her by the Jefferson Avenue school board. It was within walking distance of the school. She found the school adjacent to the church. It had a number of rooms, a fair-sized gymnasium, and a kitchen and lunchroom space. As Katrina viewed the work space and the potential it offered, she frowned in perplexity at the thought *Lord, You've taken me from one kind of teaching and put me in this situation. Is this Your way of telling me You do not need me as a dietitian?* A slight smile replaced the frown and with uplifted eyes she cried out from her heart, *I yield, Lord. I am wholly Yours. Help me as You have in the past to do this job for You Your way.*

Katrina took hold eagerly, organizing the classes, checking records, ordering supplies and textbooks. She got her assistant teachers working well with her in the plans for their classes and for the general program by treating them as a team. A friendly person, she soon made friends with people in the church. Visiting the children's homes, she gathered insights into their needs and the causes for their behavior. She gave parents ideas how they might help their children. Because of her friendly, noncondemnatory, and often helpful attitude, she became well-known and liked by adults as well as by the children.

Katrina believes that church-related schools should make a special contribution to society. It cannot happen in complete isolation from the general educational program of the rest of the people. She determined what the public schools of Rochester deemed desirable for their children and made certain that the children in her school would not be deprived of any "good thing." Making herself known at the city's educational headquarters, she asked them to put her on their mailing lists. By so doing, she received notices of all educational events planned for the public schools. Soon she received invitations to attend meetings and to listen to discussions of various programs and curriculum changes, a connection that also gave her and the Jefferson Avenue School access to all the cultural events open to the public school children.

NORTHWARD BOUND

However, she gave her highest priority to intellectual learning based upon a firm moral and religious background. She guided both teachers and students in realizing the need for continual progress. Nor did she forget the physical side of true development. Katrina helped to institute a hot lunch program, ensuring at least one hot meal per day for every child. The school placed more emphasis upon gymnastics, especially for the girls. As principal, Katrina also initiated a dress code, requiring a uniform chosen by the children. When a parent felt unable to purchase or make the uniform, she found a way. A wonderful feeling of oneness existed in the Jefferson Avenue School.

Once she found a family of girls abused by their father. The two older ones were in high school, but the younger two attended Jefferson Avenue. Katrina's own childhood experiences and her relationship with the public school system helped her get these girls the assistance they needed. The other students came to love and help them and accept them fully.

When Katrina's mother finished her Washington, D.C., assignment, she joined her daughter in Rochester. Anticipating the move, Katrina found a larger apartment some distance from the school. With help from the Brathwaite family, members of the local church, she had her furniture, still stored at Oakwood College, brought up and the place ready to move into upon her mother's arrival. Seeing what a heavy load Katrina and the other teachers carried, the older woman volunteered to teach all the language arts classes for grades five through eight. Both Margaret Earle, who taught grades five and six, and Katrina, who had grades seven and eight plus the administrative work of the school, gladly accepted the offer. The children felt special, having their teacher's mother, a doctor of education from "abroad," as their instructor. They came to their language arts classes reverently.

Late that winter Katrina's adoptive mother received an invitation to teach a summer course in the Education Department at Andrews University. At the close of the Jefferson Avenue School that year Katrina joined her mother on the Andrews campus in Berrien Springs, Michigan, where she registered for course-work toward a master's degree. After summer school both

KATRINA STANDS ALONE

returned to Rochester and to teaching in the Jefferson Avenue School. As soon as that school year ended, Katrina went into the hospital for surgery. Her mother stayed with her as long as possible, but before the younger woman had fully recuperated, she had to return to Michigan to again teach at Andrews. Mr. and Mrs. Brathwaite, now good friends, took over the care of their children's teacher. They did an excellent job, but a few days later Katrina insisted upon driving alone to Michigan. Arrangements had been made for someone to meet her half-way and complete the trip for her. Somehow, though, she and the other party missed connections, and completely exhausted but triumphant, she arrived on her own and registered for a course. Both planned to return to Rochester as soon as summer school ended. However, the dean of the Education Department offered her mother a permanent position on the staff. After a brief vacation together, Katrina returned to Rochester, and her mother to Berrien Springs.

The year went well for both of them. As soon as the spring quarter at the university ended, Katrina's mother headed for Rochester. She arrived in time for the Jefferson Avenue School closing and the graduation of its eighth graders. Many of the students hoped to continue their education in a church-related academy. For one little miss, though, it seemed financially impossible. The Brathwaites had brought her up from a toddler. They, with the help of the child's mother, had sent the girl, Irene, to the Jefferson Avenue School. Irene had always enjoyed the intimacy of a private school and dreaded attending a large public high school where she would be only a number among strangers. She brought the problem to her teacher-friend, and they prayed about it. Deeply concerned, Katrina shared the problem with her mother. "She's a wonderful youngster, talented, has a good disposition and a pleasant personality. But I fear she may not be stable enough to withstand the peer pressures of a large high school. She is so totally unspoiled."

"Yes, I've observed her," the older woman replied quietly. "Maybe, just maybe, there is a way." A long pause, then, "Do you think Irene's mother could take care of the monthly tuition?"

"Possibly," Katrina answered, wondering what could be in the back of her mother's mind.

NORTHWARD BOUND

"If so, the girl could stay with me and attend the academy on campus. As you know, I have an extra bed in my apartment and I prepare my own meals. I could just as well cook for two. And I believe I could absorb all the expenses for books, fees, and extras. Do you think Irene and her mother would accept this plan?"

Katrina jumped up, clapped her hands, then gave her mother a big hug. "Would they?" she exclaimed. "I'm sure they will. I'll contact them immediately." Then with true concern she turned from the phone to ask, "Mother, are you sure this won't be too much for you?"

"Of course not. I'll enjoy the company."

"Then it's all settled," Katrina joyfully declared as she picked up the telephone to give the news to Irene and her mother.

On a September day Irene took her first airplane ride in the care of Katrina's mother, both traveling from Rochester to Andrews University. It avoided an all-night train ride. However, they had to deplane in Chicago, more than 100 miles away from their destination. But Katrina's mother had made arrangements for Dr. and Mrs. Smith to meet them at the airport and drive them to the university campus. This proved fortuitous for Irene because she met the Smith children and had immediate campus friends. Her adjustment turned out exceptionally well.

Katrina spent that year, her fourth, as principal-teacher at the Jefferson Avenue School for the last time. She felt the need for a change of locale. Several things influenced her decision: consideration for her own financial future; the necessity to be available to care for her mother, now long past retirement age, and ailing; and the need to help with the responsibility of Irene, a lively teenager. Her conclusion—move to Berrien Springs and seek work there.

However, before she could make the move, she received a letter from Mildred Evelyn-Jones, one of her Oakwood College friends. Her daughter, Carla, would also graduate in June from Pine Forge Academy and looked forward eagerly to the possibility of continuing her education in one of the church-related colleges. How, Mildred worried, could she possibly send her daughter to college when the financial burden for her college-age son already lay heavily upon her shoulders? Could Katrina think of a way to help?

The first step, share the problem with her adoptive mother.

After a long pause, Katrina waited for her to suggest something. "I think, yes, I'm sure it'll work," the older woman said as she nodded her head in agreement with herself.

"What?"

"Carla can stay with us. We'll have to have a house. Can't pack all of us in a one-bedroom apartment."

"That'll be great! But Mother, are you sure you can handle two young girls?"

"Of course; mothers always find ways to do the necessary. You'll be available, and Carla is old enough to work part time for some of her school expenses. Living with us, there will be no charge for board and room. With whatever Mildred can add, I am sure it will work out. We're a family. Remember?"

"How could I forget? And as your daughter, I'll do all I can to help my sister, Mildred."

"Good! Let's go house-hunting."

They found a pleasant three-bedroom house not far from the university campus, all carpeted and ready for occupancy. Sending for their furniture, they moved in. Irene returned and completed work in the academy, then stayed for one year of college before leaving to pursue nursing training at a hospital and school just out of Chicago. Carla came to live with "Aunt 'Trina" and "Grandmother" until she concluded her college work with a degree in psychology. She then left to work and later do graduate studies at Western Michigan University at Kalamazoo.

When the move took place, there were no openings in Berrien Springs or other nearby towns in the church-related school system Katrina had known all her life. As a result, she applied for a position in the Benton Harbor area school system, an employer of more than 500 teachers. In less than a week she received an assignment to teach fourth grade in Benton Harbor's Bard School about 12 miles from her home base, Berrien Springs. For the first time she would teach in a public school. However, her vision and dedication to her work did not change. She would still teach to the glory of God. Parents would still be able to say as did the Brathwaites whose children attended Jefferson Avenue School in Rochester, New York:

> We thank God for the day when she [Miss Nesbitt] consented to be . . . teacher at our school. . . . We had no reservations about surrendering our children . . . to her Christian tutelage. . . . She wholeheartedly responded to the individual needs of each of our children.
> (Signed) Mrs. Arlene Braithwaite.

15

THE BARD EXPERIENCE

Katrina began to teach at the Bard Elementary School in September 1968 under the newly assigned principal, Mr. James Ray. Both were new and both eager to be successful. And both of them believed that the image of the Bard School should and could be changed. They with the other teachers and the paraprofessionals worked together for 11 years to make that transformation a reality.

It soon became evident that this new fourth-grade teacher differed significantly from many others. A certain aura set her apart. Her demeanor, attitude, and manner bespoke an inner something that controlled her. Teachers in the school began coming to her for advice. Parents noticed the improvement in their children and recommended Katrina to their relatives and friends who had or would have children for her grade level.

Her 25 years of parochial school teaching and her continued adherence to professional study had given her the insights needed for successful public school teaching. She knew who she was, what she wanted from life, and what she desired to accomplish in the classroom. To her, teaching is more than a vocation. It is her dedication to excellence for herself and for those she has the pleasure of teaching. And it is her gift to the Master Teacher. She ever keeps in mind two quotations she learned at Oakwood when taking a course entitled "Principles of Education":

"Higher than the highest human thought can reach is God's ideal for His children. Godliness—godlikeness—is the goal to be reached. Before the student there is opened a path of continual progress. He has an object to achieve, a standard to attain, that includes everything good, and pure, and noble. He will advance as fast and as far as possible in every branch of true knowledge" (E. G. White, *Education*, p. 18).

THE BARD EXPERIENCE

"The true teacher is not satisfied with second-rate work. He is not satisfied with directing his students to a standard lower than the highest which it is possible for them to attain. . . . It is his ambition to inspire them with principles of truth, obedience, honor, integrity, and purity—principles that will make them a positive force for the stability and uplifting of society" *(ibid.,* p. 29).

Sometimes people call Katrina a "hard" teacher. However, her apparent toughness is totally wrapped up in love, understanding, and devotion to her students. The superintendent of schools became aware of the desirable changes taking place at the Bard School, particularly the work of one of the fourth-grade teachers. Many of her students were surpassing those in the same grade level in more prestigious schools in the system. Intrigued that Katrina's classes, nearly all Black children, were progressing so well, he selected the Bard School as one of several to try out new programs. It began with a second language, French. Katrina's children did surprisingly well. Next he introduced a program called "Systems 80." The Department of Education offered a course for teachers to help them understand the system and how to put it to work in their classrooms. Katrina immediately volunteered to attend. She employed System 80 in the teaching of French, mathematics, reading, and language arts. Her use of it produced such good results that the educational leaders chose her as one of the taped speakers on a radio program to explain System 80 to other teachers. The next experiment dealt with computers. In a short time her entire class mastered their use so thoroughly that each child could, and usually did, make a perfect score. Quietly and efficiently she proved that her charges were capable of learning anything as well as any other group of children when loved, appreciated, and challenged.

After Katrina had served several years under Mr. Ray's principalship, the city education superintendent offered her an opportunity to become a principal. To it she replied, "Please let me stay in the classroom with the children. I do not care to assume the duties of a principal." Her decision delighted her principal. Knowing the department would approve, Mr. Ray then asked her to be a "helping-teacher" to him. This she consented

KATRINA STANDS ALONE

to do. While remaining teacher of her fourth grade, she took over the principal's duties in his absence.

When in 1979 Mr. Ray left Bard to become principal of another school, he requested that Katrina accompany him. However, she felt a sense of mission to the children of Bard School. Teaching elsewhere might be less demanding, but what would happen to her children? Would they get someone who saw only their defects and deficiencies with never a glimpse of their intellectual and inner abilities? Would her boys and girls step back into hopelessness? No, she couldn't leave them. They needed her. Some years later at her retirement, Mr. Ray gave the following testimony:

"I do remember, with a great deal of fondness, the early days at Bard Elementary School. Katrina was a brand-new teacher, eager to try out all the theories, philosophies, and tactics needed to motivate, stimulate, and if need be, devastate those occupants of desks and chairs.

"Bard School is located in a Black, low-income, inner-city neighborhood that reflects all the socioeconomic problems of troubled people. Yet, out of this school graduated people who later excelled as doctors, lawyers, teachers, famous athletes, and proud citizens of their community. Over the years the word spread in the community that, if possible, you should try to get your child in Miss Nesbitt's room. How many thousands of children has this teacher shown the beauties of art, reading, music, Black heritage, and their responsibility to be positive models to their younger siblings. How many young minds and spirits were stimulated to never be satisfied with 'just getting by.' Miss Nesbitt has not only been an inspiration to students but also to young teachers in the Benton Harbor area schools.

"Thank you, Katrina, for your understanding, patience, professionalism, and love." (Signed) James J. Ray, Principal, Northeast School.

Mrs. Ann Kennedy, who replaced Mr. Ray as Bard's principal, also found in Katrina an indispensable assistant as they worked together for four years. As a helping-teacher to the principal, Katrina shared some of the administrative duties of her principal. Mrs. Kennedy had ample time to observe and appreciate her attitudes, cooperativeness, and teaching strategies. She pays her tribute:

"During my tenure at Bard Elementary School as principal, I found the following traits of Miss Nesbitt to be outstanding: Miss Nesbitt guides the behavior of her students. The tone of her voice is *positive,* yet not demanding but firm; *calm,* yet forceful. She gives the feeling of high expectations and her assignments are carried out to completion.

"One of the most important traits that Miss Nesbitt displayed is her sensitivity to each child's needs and how these needs relate to the group as a whole. With all her experiences, she knows the developmental characteristics of each age level. She was a constant adviser and teacher-helper in the school that she taught at the longest—Bard Elementary School . . . She developed good human relationships and built healthy personalities with every new class she worked with. It was a pleasure working with Katrina Nesbitt." (Signed) Ann Kennedy, Principal, Calvin Britain School.

What Katrina had seen as a possibility when she elected to move to Michigan occurred in 1983 while she taught under Mrs. Kennedy's principalship. Katrina's mother became ill and had to be hospitalized for three months. During all that time Katrina took over the full responsibility of the home and visited her mother twice a day. In the morning she stopped by before driving to Bard 15 miles away. After a full day of teaching, she would return to the hospital where she would remain until visiting hours were over. Then at home she would correct the children's papers, complete her lesson plans for the next day, and finally get to bed in the wee hours. Her principal graciously granted her time off whenever an emergency occurred at the hospital. The entire staff, who affectionately called Katrina "Mom," did everything possible to help her during the traumatic experience. Katrina's Oakwood "sisters," Mildred E. Jones and Katie M. Soughs, came from their homes in Pennsylvania to stay for a few days and help Katrina at the house and, of course, visit Mother in the hospital. Her selfless concern for her adoptive mother epitomizes Katrina's sense of caring and devotion. They are characteristics of long duration. Pastor C. E. Moseley looks back to more than

KATRINA STANDS ALONE

40 years when he knew Katrina as a college student, and later as the teacher of his two daughters and a supervising teacher at Oakwood College. He writes:

"My best memories of Miss Nesbitt [are] of her devotion and loyalty to you [her mother]. And again I recall that she impressed me as a conscientious and consecrated person, in addition to her dedication to teaching. Few young women matched her in these." (Signed) C. E. Moseley.

Her passion for giving to the less fortunate has colored her entire life. Many a Bard student has had his or her self-esteem raised by Katrina's unobtrusive gift of clothes. With pride the children wore them and showed their appreciation by greater application to their lessons and better behavior.

Katrina had not been at Bard many years before she noticed that many of her former students and many of the neighborhood youngsters roamed about aimlessly. Most of them were too young to work. Out of school they had nothing to do. She interested some of them in becoming 4-H Club members. Lueliesse Buchanan, her efficient paraprofessional, also felt this need for the idle young people. She, with Katrina's sanction, organized some of the boys into a basketball team as a part of 4-H. Naturally the girls wanted to be included. Lue assembled them into a cheerleading team and marching band. Other girls wanted something quieter. Katrina and another fourth-grade teacher, Maxisure Garrett, set up a craft program for them. When not involved with the basketball and cheerleading groups, Lueliesse also helped with the crafts. Rodney Tripplet, a teacher, and one of the custodians, Benjamin Marlow, gave valuable assistance, coaching the basketball team and the cheerleading squad. When these two groups were idle, many of both the boys and the girls felt free to join in with the crafts group.

While the 4-H projects revolved around Katrina, we must also commend Lue, Rodney, and Ben for the fine sportsmanship of the ball players and the spotless appearance and marching precision of the cheerleaders. The crafts produced by the young people under the instruction of Maxisure and Katrina won many ribbons, awards, and special mention at the county and 4-H fairs each year. Some of the 4-H'ers who had gone on to high school

THE BARD EXPERIENCE

and were ready to graduate asked to work with Katrina as helpers. They wanted to share with others what she had so generously given to them.

Katrina spent her last three years at Bard under the able leadership of Principal Renee Williams. Bard had long since been reduced from a K-8 to a preschool and K-4, greatly reducing its enrollment. The Martindale School, not far from Bard, had only grades five and six. Since the quota in neither school warranted a full-time principal, Mrs. Williams served both schools. But because Martindale absorbed much of her time, Bard often had to depend upon Katrina, who still held the status of helper-teacher. Like her predecessors, Ray and Kennedy, Principal Williams found her indispensable.

Children may be promoted from Katrina's classroom but never from her heart. As far as possible she follows their achievements from grade to grade, attends their high school graduation exercises, visits them when hospitalized, and attends the wake or funeral when death snatches away one of "her" children or a member of their families.

After 18 years of loving and working for Bard's children and its community, she felt the need for rest. For 43 years she had tried through her teaching, example, and association to educate and uplift those committed to her care. For two years she had been talking about retiring. The time had now come to do it.

16

HONORS FOR A SUPER TEACHER

Once assured that as of June 6, 1986, Miss Katrina Nesbitt would definitely retire, Bard School, the board of education, and fellow teachers and paraprofessionals all began planning how best to honor her. At a meeting held in her absence, Principal Williams and her teachers and staff unanimously agreed to observe May 27 in their school as Miss Katrina Nesbitt's Day. They made their plans for celebration with great secrecy. Katrina sensed something unusual as children looked at her strangely and little groups of teachers stopped talking as she approached them, but when she asked, "What's going on?" the children would respond with giggles and the teachers with "You know, the usual" or "Nothing much" or "Just talking to be talking."

She knew that it involved her somehow. But what? When her curiosity reached fever point, a teacher approached her and said, "Mom, we hate to lose you. Before you retire, we would like to do something for you. Will you have breakfast with us on May 27? We'll come for you. You won't have to drive yourself in that early."

Katrina surmised that there would be more than a breakfast involved. She graciously accepted the invitation, and when the time came dressed for it with care. Reasoning the breakfast would be the key to all the recent secrecy, she also took another outfit with her. Before 7:00 a.m. the morning of May 27 a limousine arrived at her home to take her to the special breakfast at a local restaurant. All then drove to the school, talking and laughing. Katrina entered the main hall of the school as one of the teachers held the door open for her. Once inside she momentarily stood in shock, for on the main bulletin board that usually

HONORS FOR A SUPER TEACHER

displayed children's work or announcements large letters now spelled out "Katrina Nesbitt Day!" As she recovered and started down the long hall toward her classroom, two of her colleagues stood in front of her and told her, "Not today; no classroom for you," and gently led her into the principal's office.

With a worried frown she asked, "But what am I supposed to do?"

They answered, "Just follow directions. You'll be told what to do." As they left they suggested, "You might take a nap in the teachers' lounge."

That idea appealed to her, but the lounge reeked with stale cigarette smoke, surely not a place for a nonsmoker to rest. She went to the nurses' quarters, where they found her at lunchtime when they brought her a hugh salad lunch.

After lunch a second-grade boy, dressed in his best suit, escorted Katrina into the assembly room, decorated for the occasion. Her eyes bulged as she saw first the eyes of all the children and the teachers focused on her. Then she gasped when she glanced at the stage and saw her name blazed across the stage: "Katrina Nesbitt Day." Along the long side walls similar letters repeated her name. Her young escort pulled her gently toward the stage and to a chair reserved for her. She followed mechanically like a robot. Always she had tried to remain in the background while she pushed her children forward. Now as she viewed the sea of faces, looking up expectantly at her, she wanted to do what frightened little girls do in such a situation—run away. But she could not. The smiles and shining eyes said clearly, "We love you and want to show you how much."

Each grade had made a collective gift and now presented it. The preschoolers sang "You Are My Sunshine" before giving her a sunshine face covered with pictures they had made. The little boy who brought it to her liked it so well that he did not want to part with it. However, a hug and a kiss from Katrina loosened his grasp and brought out a big smile. The kindergartners also made a sunshine face as their gift. The more sophisticated first graders had colored individual pictures and mounted them on a large board suitable for hanging on a wall. The second graders compiled a book of traced and colored hands to illustrate the maxim "Put them together and they spell SUPER TEACHER." The third graders used a similar idea but artistically traced and colored hands on a large white heart. Miss Nesbitt's fourth graders, unknown to her, went a step farther with the traced-and-crayoned-hands idea. They put their signed pieces of art on muslin blocks which the preschool teacher assembled into a quilt. Not a word of any of the activities had leaked out to Katrina. Who says children can't keep a secret? In addition to their handiwork, the children and their parents made up a purse of more than $100.

The children, teachers, and friends also expressed their deep feelings with cards containing appropriate messages such as:

"You make the world a better place . . . Thank you."

"You're the most special teacher in the whole world. You are like a pretty pearl." Some sixth graders who had been Miss Nesbitt's pupils two years earlier but now attended another school brought a card with the message:

"Thank you for loving us in spite of our shortcomings, for counting on us and sharing our lives, for making us feel the most important persons in the world. Thank you for being you.—With love and best wishes, Fourth Grade Class of 1984."

But Bard had not finished paying tribute. At 3:30 its teachers and others they had invited, including Katrina's mother, gave a second program of music, brief speeches, and a demonstration by some of the cheerleading group who had also performed during the earlier program. Katrina received two plaques; one from the Bard staff, the other from a successful teacher in the system whom Katrina had helped when he began his teaching career. But plaques were not enough. As another way of saying "We'll miss you; please don't forget us," the Bard staff and some parents gave her a silver dessert server. The ceremony ended with the planting of a redbud tree on Bard's front lawn as a perpetual memorial to a favorite teacher.

Although Katrina had been in school all day, her children had had a substitute teacher. Did it mean their teacher's retirement had already begun? Some of the children remained after dismissal to talk it over. To them every evidence pointed to "no more Miss Nesbitt as our teacher." Tears welled up and spilled over.

HONORS FOR A SUPER TEACHER

Someone passed by the room and heard the weeping. Concerned, this person reported to Katrina, "Miss Nesbitt, you better go to your room. Those kids are crying their eyes out!"

Before she was halfway down the long hall to her classroom, one of her girls, red-eyed and sniffling, met her and questioned, "Miss Nesbitt, who's going to be our substitute tomorrow?"

"Why I am," she consoled.

"You are?" Eyes brightened, the girl ran back to the classroom and proclaimed happily, "Miss Nesbitt's goin' to teach us tomorrow!"

"She is!" the little group chorused joyously. By that time Katrina entered the room.

"Yes, you can't get rid of me until school closes." With open arms they rushed up and hugged her.

"Now go home. I'll see you in the morning."

"Yes, Miss Nesbitt," they said simultaneously.

Katrina watched them leave, then went back to the assembly room. At home that evening she had a chance to read the messages on carefully selected cards. Maxisure, the other fourth-grade teacher at Bard, had written:

"Miss Nesbitt is one person I admire. She is kind, considerate, and concerned about everyone."—Maxisure Garrett. Another teacher said it this way:

"I remember Miss Nesbitt's relationship with her students. She cared for them but did not spoil them. She taught them skills not in the textbooks. Most of all, she gave her love to her students."—Daniel Ellerbrook. Teacher Betty Green Moore penned the following:

"My time at Bard was very special. One of the reasons is a beautiful lady named Miss Nesbitt. . . . I'm glad our paths crossed because I know I am a better professional because of it."

Perhaps a card signed by all the Bard teachers expressed the general feelings:

"You have a wonderful way of going out of your way to be wonderful."

Two days later on May 29, the Benton Harbor Education Association entertained all the year's retirees at a dinner at the Plaza Inn. Each of the retiring ladies, including Katrina, received

KATRINA STANDS ALONE

a silver candy dish. A former teacher in the system, unable to attend the May 27 occasion at Bard, sent a mailogram to the Benton Harbor Education Association to be read at the general celebration on May 29. In part it stated:

"Thanks to your superb leadership and training as a master teacher, I am able to teach and touch the lives of many children. . . . You deserve this . . . retirement celebration because of your dedication, commitment, loyalty, and concern for all those you have touched. We love you, Miss Nesbitt. Thank you for lifting us to higher heights."—Viola Watson.

On the following Wednesday, not to be left out, the paraprofessionals, former student teachers, and others who had worked with or under Katrina banded together and entertained her at a dinner held at a local Holiday Inn banquet room. They presented her with a beautiful engraved silver tray.

The next day, June 5, the yearly banquet for all retirees in the system took place in the Commons Room of the Benton Harbor High School. Each retiree received a Cross gold pen and pencil set as he or she responded by telling the number of years served in the system. The program climaxed with the announcement of the Teacher of the Year 1985-1986, a custom instituted during the school year 1978-1979. Out of more than 500 teachers, Katrina Nesbitt had become Benton Harbor area school system's first Teacher of the Year. She had received a citation and a plaque bearing the inscription:

1978-1979
OUTSTANDING TEACHER OF THE YEAR
KATRINA V. NESBITT
IN APPRECIATION
FOR YOUR DEDICATION
AND FAITHFUL SERVICE
TO THE STUDENTS OF
BENTON HARBOR AREA SCHOOLS
BENTON HARBOR BOARD OF EDUCATION

Each year thereafter Katrina's name came up for the honor until, in fairness to the other teachers, the system decided her name could not be proposed for the honor.

HONORS FOR A SUPER TEACHER

In addition to being an excellent teacher, Katrina knows how to work with the parentally or socially abused child. The experiences of her own childhood and youth helped her to empathize with disadvantaged and often abused children. Her efforts to walk in the steps of the Master Teacher have made her the perpetual Teacher of the Year in the hearts of the Benton Harbor community.

Joseph A. Shurn, Ed. D., director of personnel, offered the following testimonial upon her retirement:

"May I express the appreciation of the board of education, the administration, the staff, and the community for your many years of faithful service. I know you have played an important role in the lives of the students who have played under your supervision and guidance."—Sincerely, Joseph A. Shurn.

Mama Lois's often repeated prognosis that an inherited lack of moral excellence in her grandchild would bring added dishonor upon the Nesbitt name, backfired. Instead the little child, despised and often abused both physically and emotionally by her grandmother, has come to high honor. Wherever she is known, the name Katrina Nesbitt is held in great respect. She leaves a shining trail for others to follow.